FAMILY, FOOD AND THE FRIARS

Experience the Richness of Italian Cuisine through Cultivating, Cutting, Cooking and Consuming with Those you Love

Family, Food and the Friars: Experience the Richness of Italian Cuisine Through Cultivating, Cutting, Cooking and Consuming with Those You Love

By Gino Barbaro

Chef & Owner of Gino's Trattoria and Gino's Family

Second edition

Editor: Amy Kelley

Photographs: Kathleen Maffetone and Julia Barbaro

 Megan Fletcher p. 183

Cover Design: Kristin Gawley

Ginjules Publishing

ISBN-13: 978-1511833615

ISBN-10: 1511833610

Dedicated to the Franciscan Friars of the Renewal

Twenty percent of all profits from this book are being donated to the friars to help combat poverty and hunger.

CONTENTS

How to use this book...

The intention of this book is to illustrate how to involve the entire family in the cooking process. We want the reader to use the cook book in conjunction with our website. Every section includes a resource page that can be accessed at http://FamilyFoodandtheFriars.com/resources that includes tips and videos on the content presented. The recipes themselves also include resource links that can be visited to watch the videos on executing the recipes. Our website ginosfamily. com is chock-full of tips and articles on gardening and cooking with your children, as well as resources on shopping for produce and useful articles on parenting.

INTRODUCTION

I felt compelled to write this cookbook for several reasons. I wanted the Franciscan Friars and any beginner cooks to have a simple and easy-to-read cookbook at their disposal. I also had a desire to share my love for food, especially the eating part.

Food is still an essential part of our lives and many families are missing out on wonderful mealtime experiences because they are intimidated about cooking. My wife Julia and I created *Gino's family* with the concept of teaching parents to cook along side their children and then sit down at the dinner table to enjoy a family meal. We have been blessed with 6 wonderful children who are an integral part of our lives.. When you visit our website, http://FamilyFoodandtheFriars.com, you will have access to all of our garden and cooking videos, as well as countless articles on cooking and parenting.

We are all born with certain gifts in life, and I wanted to share my gifts: cooking and teaching. I've been cooking practically my whole life – I started working at my father's pizzeria in Yonkers when I was eight, and I've owned an Italian restaurant, Gino's Trattoria in Mahopac, NY, for more than 20 years now.

I began teaching some Franciscan postulants, young men who are contemplating joining the Franciscan Friars of the Renewal (CFRs), how to cook in 2005.

The friars are a Catholic religious order who assume a life of poverty and renounce all worldly possessions in pursuit of aiding the poor and underprivileged. They choose to live in destitute neighborhoods and bring comfort to all who come knocking at their door. These men are truly extraordinary examples of what is important in this life.

The initial stage in becoming a member of the Franciscan Friars is called postulancy, meaning a time of questioning. The postulants are like freshmen friars. They live at the friary for a 10-month experience of everything Franciscan. During this time they are praying and discerning if they are called to take the next step in joining the friars as novices. Most postulants have very little experience in the kitchen, and I was invited down to Harlem from our home in Mahopac by Father Luke Fletcher to teach them how to cook.

Writing this cookbook has allowed me to thank the CFR's, especially Fr. Luke, for welcoming my family with open arms and showing us the true meaning of life and the importance of helping others in need. My family is eternally grateful for their love and prayers.

For more information about the friars, visit franciscanfriars.com. If you would like to send a donation visit http://franciscanfriars.com/donate.

Many recipes that are written in this book have their own stories, and I accompany many recipes with a small narrative. My hope is to help the reader understand why certain ingredients are used in each dish and instill the desire and passion to follow through with the recipe. Each recipe can be used as a template; the better you become as a cook, the more of yourself you can add to each recipe and the more creative you can become.

It may seem odd that you come across recipes in this cookbook that are not Italian. The friars do not have the luxury of shopping for their food and rely on donations to fill their pantry. You may also stumble upon them at the produce market in the city begging for any leftover produce that is poised to land in the trashcan. I have included recipes such as guacamole and barbecue sauce, to give them (and you) the knowledge of how to use different ingredients while still trying to inject an Italian flair.

Buon Appetito!

Gino Barbaro

GB

FOREWORD

What began as a simple request for some much-needed help has developed into a wonderful tradition.

I am the postulant director for my order, the Franciscan Friars of the Renewal. Like myself when I joined the friars, some of the postulants are culinary-challenged!

Entrusted with the training of our beginning brothers, I timidly reached out to Gino for help. With my fingers crossed I asked him, "Would you be available to teach the postulants some basics in the kitchen?" I am not sure if Gino and his family were aware of all that would follow from the generous "yes" he offered (as is his nature).

Having never cooked before, I only knew how to boil water and toast toast. There was a lot to learn along the way. I am still no Gino Barbaro, yet all of these years later no one has died from my dinners.

Sharing faith, friendship and food, the Barbaro family has been such a blessing to our little community and our little neighborhood in the Hamilton Heights section of Harlem. Gino truly has the gifts of cooking and teaching. Although we friars are called to the vocation of religious life, we need the example and encouragement of the vocation to family life.

Not only has Gino improved the eating experience at the friary, he has inspired us in our outreach to our neighbors. When the word goes out that the Barbaros are cooking for our lunch program, affectionately called Saint Joseph's Table, the room is packed with eager diners.

Thanks also to their help, our neighborhood Thanksgiving dinners have become legendary. Something very beautiful has developed, like a page right out of the Gospel. We are often reminded of our Father, who provides our daily bread through such willing instruments as we try to be a blessing to others.

How many times do we see Jesus sharing a meal in the Gospels? And Saint Francis wanted his friars to gather around the table of the Lord's altar in prayer and the table of fellowship in fraternity. Remember that he was Italian – meals together are important!

Now that you know a little of the backstory of this book, enjoy all of the wonderful recipes and anecdotes. I hope that they help you to draw closer to your family in faith as well as create many mouth-watering memories! Thank you, Gino and Julia and family.

Fr. Luke Mary Fletcher, CFR

BASICS

This is where Gino's Family incorporates the 4 Cs, cultivating, cutting, cooking and consuming. We feel that it is imperative to master the basics of cooking. We have included an entire gardening section (cultivate) to commence the cooking process. There is a section on knife skills (cut), along with techniques of cooking (cook). Refer back to this chapter when a question arises on ingredients or methods of cooking. Finally, you will be able to assess when food is properly cooked and what temperature certain foods should be prepared (consume).

KNIFE SKILLS

It is imperative that you begin with very sharp knives. You are more likely to cut yourself with a dull knife because you will be forcing the knife through the meat or vegetable. Using a sharp knife allows a cook to be more fluid and much quicker. When you are cutting, always cut down and away from you.

Please store your knives so the blades are protected (a knife block is best). You do not want them mixed with other utensils or you will end up nicking the blades. Do not use your knives on metal or plastic laminate countertops, only on soft surfaces such as butcher blocks or composite cutting boards.

You can use a sharpening steel to remove any burrs or nicks from your knife. To use a sharpening steel, hold the knife at a 20-degree angle and direct the knife up and then down the steel. This only realigns the blade and smooths out any nicks. If there is no improvement, have them sharpened by a professional. I have been using Ambrosi Cutlery in Putnam County, NY for over 15 years. You can send your knives UPS and they will return them beautifully sharpened.

TYPES OF KNIVES

Bread Knife A serrated knife used primarily to cut bread.

Chef Knife One of the most important knives in the kitchen. It can be used to perform all types of chopping and dicing as well as flattening garlic. I like to use a chef knife that has a length of 10 inches.

Paring Knife A small versatile knife that comes in handy when all other knives are being used. It is perfect for coring fruit and chopping fruits and vegetables.

Filet Knife This knife has a long thin blade. It is used to clean skin off of fish, as well as cleaning cuts of meat such as veal and beef. I like to use the filet knife when removing the fat from meat.

Boning Knife This knife is a bit short and used to remove filets of fish or cuts of meat from the bone.

Cleaver A heavy blade used to chop through animal bones.

MEASUREMENTS

The following are some basic measurements and conversions to serve as a reference.

Dash	=	1/8 teaspoon
3 teaspoons	=	1 tablespoon
2 tablespoons	=	1 fl. oz.
4 tablespoons	=	1/4 cup (2 fl. oz.)
8 tablespoons	=	1/2 cup (4 fl. oz.)
16 tablespoons	=	1 cup (8 fl. oz.)
2 cups	=	1 pint (16 fl. oz.)
2 pints	=	1 quart (32 fl. oz.)
4 quarts	=	1 gallon (128 fl. oz.)
1 pound	=	16 oz.

TEMPERATURES FOR COOKED MEATS

There are several precautions to take when preparing food. Cook food to the desired temperature and make sure to cool the food rapidly before placing in the refrigerator. Use an ice bath to cool all stocks and sauces. Your refrigerator should be set between 38-42 degrees to slow the growth of bacteria. Always cover food with lids or plastic film to prevent the absorption of odors and cross contamination of other foods.

Here are the suggested temperatures to cook meat to the desired level.

	Rare	Medium Rare	Medium	Well Done
Chicken				160
Lamb	130-135	140-145	150	160
Turkey				160
Beef	125-130	135	140	160
Pork			150	160

Sautéing Rapidly cooking small pieces of food over high heat in oil or some other type of fat. The three keys to sautéing are: high heat, uniform cut of food and constant movement.

The goal is to brown the food on all sides while using very little oil in a shallow sauté pan. Once the food is browned, it is removed and the pan is deglazed with some type of liquid, preferably wine, stock or water. Deglazing the pan removes the caramelized bits of food from the bottom of the pan. These bits will aid in creating a delicious sauce.

Grilling Cooking over an open fire on top of a grid of metal bars while using either gas, wood, electric, or charcoal. It is one of the oldest methods of cooking and one of my favorites. You can grill not only fish, meat and chicken, but also roast peppers and other vegetables. You can even grill pizza.

Braising A method of cooking by which the food is first browned, then placed in a small amount of liquid and cooked at low heat for a long period of time. The slow cooking allows the food to tenderize and develop flavor. I prefer to braise food in the oven.

Steaming Placing food in a basket or on a rack above boiling water inside a covered pan. This gentle cooking method allows the food to retain its shape and many of the vitamins and minerals.

Cooking pasta Never add oil to the boiling water. Never rinse pasta once it is cooked. This will wash off the starch from the pasta and will make it nearly impossible for your sauce to stick to the pasta. Use a large pot of salted, boiling water so you will be able to stir the pasta and prevent it from sticking to the pot. Make sure to stir the pasta frequently, especially during the first couple of minutes.

There is a term that the French use: mise en place. Translated, it means 'everything in its place.'

In my kitchen, I use different color cutting boards for meats and vegetables: red for meat, white for bread, yellow for vegetables and brown for fish. This greatly decreases the risk of cross contamination amongst foods.

When you begin to attack a recipe, make sure that you have all the ingredients measured and cut. You do not want to begin sautéing and then realize you forgot to dice your chicken. This will throw off your timing and will disrupt your thought process.

Finally, while you are cooking, clean up after yourself so you are not left with a mess when you finish cooking. There are few things in life that can ruin a great meal; a sink full of dishes and pots is one of them.

GLOSSARY

BEANS

Cannellini Bean Also called a white kidney bean, this bean is available dry or canned. I use them for Pasta & Fagioli and Escarole & Bean soups.

Chickpeas Most commonly used in soups, salads and stews, chickpeas are a source of protein. I prefer to use canned because dried chickpeas take a long time to cook. I use them in Minestrone Soup and Bean Salad.

Lentil This legume is dried when it has ripened. Add to soups and stews, cook just until tender.

Split pea The color of this bean varies from pale green to yellow and it derives its name from the drying process that 'splits' the pea.

Preparing dried beans Soak beans overnight to soften. Discard water. Add 1 pound beans into 2 quarts fresh water, 1 garlic clove and 2 bay leaves. Bring to a boil and simmer for 1 ½ hours or until beans begin to soften, keeping them al dente. Remove from stove, add salt and cool.

Cooking tip Adding salt at end of cooking allows bean to become tender.

OILS

Extra virgin olive oil The first cold pressing of the olive, which yields a fruity flavorful oil. Use this expensive oil to sauté food and to prepare dressings. Store in a cool dark place.

Virgin olive oil Also a first press oil, but it contains a slightly higher level of acidity. Still a very good quality oil.

Vegetable oil, soybean and canola These are popular oils for frying because of their high smoking point. Do not use for salad dressing because they have little flavor.

HERBS AND SPICES

In Italian cuisine, we tend to use herbs more than spices. When using fresh herbs, chop them right before using them; otherwise they will lose their pungency and flavor.

Parsley A very popular and versatile herb. I like to use the flat leaf type, called Italian parsley, which has more flavor. Used in sauces, meats, chicken, fish, salads.

Basil Most renowned for making pesto, this herb is delicate and will discolor quickly once it is cut. Tear the leaves by hand when using in uncooked dishes such as Mozzarella & Roasted Peppers.

Thyme Used often with lamb and chicken as well as tomato sauces.

Sage A very pungent herb used to flavor pork and chicken. I use sage when I prepare Veal Saltimbocca; one leaf is placed between the veal and a slice of prosciutto.

Salt The most commonly used seasoning in the world. I prefer to use sea salt due to its health benefits. Salts are used to flavor foods as well as to preserve them, and appears to heighten their flavors. Always under salt your dishes then add more while eating.

Cilantro This herb is very similar in appearance to parsley, but not in taste. It is used in many Latin American and Chinese dishes. It's great in guacamole and bean salads.

Pepper I use two varieties at the restaurant: white and black. White pepper is less pungent and not visible in dishes, allowing me to conceal its appearance but not its flavor. The best way to use pepper is to keep it whole in a pepper mill and grind it as needed.

Cinnamon The inner bark of a tropical evergreen tree. It can be purchased either in sticks or powdered. It's used primarily in sweet dishes.

Nutmeg Primarily used as a baking spice, nutmeg can also be used in cream sauce and potato dishes and can be bought ground or whole. I prefer to buy whole and grate when needed.

Cayenne A pepper that is finely ground and adds a depth of flavor and spice to any dish. When using cayenne, use sparingly due to its potency.

Paprika A powder made from ground, sweet red pepper pods. The flavor of the spice ranges from mild to hot, and the color from light to dark red. Paprika can be used as a seasoning or a garnish.

CHEESE

Mozzarella A soft cheese made from cow's milk. It's very popular on pizza and as a topping on chicken and sandwiches.

Ricotta This cheese, made from the whey of cow's milk, is moist and creamy. I use it as a stuffing for chicken rollatini, manicotti and lasagna as well as Italian cheesecake.

Gorgonzola A moist, creamy cheese that is injected with mold spores. This cheese pairs well with walnuts, apples and pears. It can also be used in a cream sauce for chicken or pasta.

Parmiggiano Reggiano This is a delicious cheese produced in the northern regions of Italy. Authentic Parmigiano Reggiano is aged for at least one year and is used as a grating cheese. It can also be sliced and eaten. It is best to grate this cheese and combine it with pecorino to combine the sweetness of parmigiano and the saltiness of Pecorino Romano cheese.

Pecorino This is a hard cheese made from sheep's milk. It is aged for at least six months and can be eaten as table cheese or grated for pasta.

Provolone A spicy, hard, cow's milk cheese that is delicious with cold cuts.

Goat Cheese White, creamy cheese derived from goat milk that possesses a slightly tart flavor. I like to use goat cheese on salads and as a topping for pizza.

FRUITS AND VEGETABLES

ORGANIC FRUITS AND VEGETABLES

I am a big proponent of buying and growing organic foods.

I recommend buying organic: apples, bell peppers, celery, peaches, pears, potatoes, spinach, strawberries, nectarines, raspberries and cherries.

This group of foods is not as affected by pesticides: bananas, kiwi, mango, papaya pineapple, asparagus, avocado, broccoli, cauliflower, garlic, onions, and peas.

GARDENING

FamilyFoodandtheFriars.com

My family loves to garden and we use no pesticides or chemicals in the garden. We rotate our crops and introduce Japanese beetles to reduce the pests in the garden.

If you would like any information on home gardening, please visit our website familyfoodandthefriars.com and ginosfamily.com go to the video section. There you will be able to view the steps of gardening beginning with early spring and progressing through the entire growing season. All the videos feature my children planting vegetables, pulling weeds, watering, and, of course, eating their hard work. It is a great way to teach children responsibility, as well as healthy eating, while having fun outdoors.

You will be amazed at how easy it is to grow your own vegetables. If you feel overwhelmed, start with a couple of pots the first year, and then progress to a larger garden the following year. Remember, we need to learn how to walk before we can run.

A vegetable garden planner is essential if you want to set up your vegetable garden in the most efficient and attractive way. You will be able to harvest many more delicious vegetables for your kitchen if you have taken some time to plan your garden before you start. I draw a sketch of the garden with my children and let them choose the location of all plants. I even designate a raised bed to each little one to give them a sense of responsibility, and a feeling of achievement once they pick the first vegetable.

There is not a one-size-fits-all vegetable garden planner because every garden is a little different. Your soil type, climate and the amount of sun, shade and shelter in your garden will all play a part in determining which are the best vegetables for you to grow and where to locate them in your garden. However, you can use the hints and tips in this article to construct your own vegetable garden planner.

If you are planting vegetables within a bigger garden that also contains flowering plants and trees, then you can simply pick a good place for each vegetable according to whether they like sun or shade, etc.

On the other hand if you have a dedicated vegetable plot, there are some points to consider when you are deciding on its location, as well as the location of individual plants within it. Most vegetables like to have some sunlight but not to be in constant full sun.

Many plants require a lot of water in order to grow big, healthy vegetable crops, so one principle of your vegetable garden planner might be to site your plot near to a faucet. If you do not have a faucet in your garden, you could grow your vegetables in a place that can be reached by a hose from your kitchen window.

You can also consider companion planting. This is a system of planting vegetables beside others that are mutually supportive. It may seem weird that plants can support each other, but they do, usually by repelling certain pests. The best known example is the 'three sisters': squash, maize and climbing beans. There are many other examples too, such as the allium family (onions, garlic, leeks) with the nightshade family (tomatoes, peppers, potatoes, eggplant), the brassica family (cabbage, broccoli, cauliflower) and carrots.

Square foot gardening is a popular option for many new vegetable gardens. This usually involves raised or ground-level beds of 4 ft width, divided into one foot squares, with a different vegetable in each square. Depending on the size of the plant, some plants will need a whole square for each, and others will happily grow two, four or more to a square foot. Having the beds only 4 ft wide allows you to reach everything. If you want a bigger vegetable garden, it is best to create paths between beds so that you have good access to your plants for weeding, harvesting and other tasks.

Do not forget to rotate the vegetables in your garden. This is essential for preventing many diseases from becoming established. For example, if you always grow tomatoes in the same place, the fungal and other diseases that tend to attack tomatoes will gradually gain in strength over the years until they become a real problem in that spot. By constructing your vegetable garden planner in a way that will allow you to move your tomatoes each year, you can prevent this. I draw sketches of my garden every year and keep them to remind me what was planted in each bed the previous year.

FRUITS AND VEGETABLES

It is important that you use produce that is in season. The produce will cost much less and possess a superior flavor.

Whenever fruit is served, it should be taken out of the refrigerator and brought to room temperature. Below is some important storage advice for commonly used fruits and vegetables.

Apples They are one of my favorite fruits; they should be refrigerated to prolong their freshness.

Bananas Never refrigerate. Due to their delicate nature, they will turn black.

Lemons Citrus fruits can be left on top of the counter but if you refrigerate them, you will increase their shelf life.

Mango The refrigerator will kill the taste. Leave them out on the counter and peel when you are ready to eat.

Melons and Pineapples Only place these fruits in the refrigerator once they are cut.

Mushrooms Place them in a dark, cool place to lengthen their shelf life.

Onions The flavor of an onion gets stronger the older the onion gets. Keep onions in the refrigerator if you do not want to shed tears when you cut them. The oil from the onion will be less intense.

Potatoes Leaving potatoes at room temperature facilitates the transfer of sugars in the potato to starch, which gives it its flavor.

Tomatoes The taste of a ripe, juicy tomato will disappear in the fridge.

BASIC SAUCES

MOST SAUCES NOWADAYS CAN BE BOUGHT ALREADY PREPARED IN GROCERY STORES OR EVEN RESTAURANTS.

WE HAVE MANY CUSTOMERS WHO BUY OUR VODKA AND MARINARA SAUCES TO TAKE OUT.

IT IS IMPORTANT THAT YOU MASTER THESE BASIC SAUCES BECAUSE IT IS MUCH CHEAPER FOR YOU TO PREPARE THEM AND YOU WILL BE ABLE TO CREATE AND CONTROL THE FLAVORS TO SUIT YOUR PERSONAL PREFERENCES.

THESE SAUCES ACT AS A BASE FOR YOUR COOKING, AND IF THEIR TASTE IS UNAPPEALING, THEN NO MATTER HOW SUCCULENT YOUR DISH IS, IT WILL BE WASTED.

FORTUNATELY, WITH A LITTLE PRACTICE, YOU CAN BECOME A PRO AT PREPARING THESE SAUCES.

CHICKEN STOCK

The goal in any kitchen should be to eliminate waste and reuse as much as possible. Use the skins of onions, carrot peels, parsley stems, and celery leaves as an addition when making your stock.* Make sure to cut your vegetables around 2 inches in size so that they do not dissolve when they have been simmering for a long period of time.

Makes two gallons

5 pounds chicken bones

2 onions

4 stalks of celery

2 carrots

1 tablespoon peppercorn

8 dry bay leaves

1 tablespoon salt

1 bunch of parsley stems

2½ gallons of water

Place all ingredients in a large stock pot, bring to a boil and let simmer for 3-4 hours, stirring occasionally. You want to achieve a slow simmer, which will allow the stock to reduce and strengthen in flavor.

When complete, remove from the stove and pass through a strainer into a large container. It is important to cool the stock quickly to avoid bacteria growth. When cooled, place in the refrigerator.

Tip: Reuse the carcasses of a roasted chicken to make your stock.

*This is called mirepoix, a combination of vegetables — usually onions, carrots, and celery — that is used to flavor stocks. The ratio is: two parts onion, one part celery, one part carrot.

DEMI-GLACE

My brother and I commonly refer to demi-glace as 'brown sauce.'

This sauce acts as a base for dishes ranging from our Chicken Francese to Pork Chops Campagnola. If you find this recipe too time-consuming, you can always buy demi-glace in specialty grocery stores or call Gino's Trattoria and we will ship our sauce to your home.

Make sure to prepare a large quantity and freeze whatever is left over for future use. You can pour the sauce into ice cube trays, and when they have frozen, remove them from the tray and place into sealable plastic bags. Each ice cube size is sufficient for one portion of a recipe.

Makes 1 gallon

10 pounds veal bones
3 carrots, chopped into 2-inch pieces
4 stalks celery, cut into 2-inch pieces
2 onions, chopped into 2-inch pieces
1 cup red wine

1 sprig parsley stems
1/2 cup tomato paste
6 bay leaves
1 tablespoon black peppercorns
2½ gallons cold water
2 tablespoons salt (more as needed)

ROUX

Heat oven to 500°F. Roast the bones until lightly browned, about 1½ hours.

Add carrot, celery and onion and spread evenly. Roast until vegetables and bones are deeply colored, about 45 minutes. Deglaze the pan with 1 cup of red wine. Transfer bones and vegetables to a 20-quart stock pot. Scrape bits from roasting pan and add to stock pot. Add parsley sprig, tomato paste, bay leaves, and peppercorn. Fill stock pot with 2½ gallons cold water, about 2 inches from top. Allow stock to come to a boil and reduce to a simmer. Stock should simmer for at least 4 hours, but we allow our stock to simmer for 6 hours at the restaurant to achieve a deeper, richer flavor. Skim fat from stock.

Strain stock and return to a sauce pot. Reheat stock and begin to add roux slowly. Make sure stock is not overly hot and add a small amount of roux while constantly stirring. Bring stock up to a boil briefly, and then remove from heat. If your sauce develops any lumps, pass it through a strainer.

CLASSIC VINAIGRETTE

Making your own salad dressing is very simple, yet the recipe is versatile.

The basic proportions for a classic vinaigrette are as follows:

Makes 1 cup

- 1 tablespoon shallots
- 3 tablespoons vinegar
- 1 tablespoon Dijon mustard
- 12 tablespoons oil
- Salt & pepper to taste

I like to add chopped shallots to my vinaigrette to impart sweetness. The Dijon mustard acts as an emulsifier and allows the oil and vinegar to blend together. When choosing a vinegar, try to pair the vinegar with the lettuce in the recipe. For example, the sweetness of balsamic vinegar contrasts well with the bitterness of arugula and adds complexity to the salad. There are also countless oils you can use, such as walnut, almond or hazelnut.

To prepare any vinaigrette, mince shallots and mix with vinegar and mustard in a bowl. Using a blender or whisking in a bowl by hand, drizzle oil slowly into mixture, and watch vinaigrette start to thicken. Salt & pepper to taste.

Honey Dijon Add one tablespoon of honey to vinaigrette. Add 1/2 teaspoon extra of Dijon mustard for more flavor.

Raspberry Substitute raspberry vinegar for red wine vinegar. This vinegar is excellent with bitter leafy greens.

Blue Cheese Mince one shallot and mix with 2 tablespoons each of cider vinegar and Dijon mustard. Using a blender or whisking in a bowl by hand, drizzle 1/2 cup oil slowly into mixture, and watch vinaigrette start to thicken. As a final step, fold in chives and blue cheese until incorporated. Salt & pepper to taste.

BARBECUE SAUCE

The key to a delicious barbecue sauce is the balance between its spiciness and sweetness. Italians rarely use this sauce. Their preference is to simply marinate the meat with olive oil, rosemary, lemon, and herbs. That being said, I feel every cook should have a barbecue sauce recipe. Store-bought barbecue sauce can be expensive and contain unnecessary and unhealthy ingredients.

Makes 5 cups

1¼ cup ketchup

1 cup honey

2¾ cup oil

1 tablespoon dry mustard

3/4 cup vinegar

2 teaspoons fresh ginger, peeled and diced

5 tablespoons Worcestershire sauce

Mix all ingredients thoroughly.

BLACKENED SPICE RUB

FamilyFoodandtheFriars.com

This spice rub can be mixed together and stored away in an airtight container for up to six months. I like to add fresh parsley right before I incorporate it into the recipe. At the restaurant, we use this rub on salmon, tuna, chicken, scallops and even shrimp. If the recipe is too spicy, add less cayenne pepper.

Makes 1/2 cup

1 teaspoon cayenne pepper

1 teaspoon black pepper

2 tablespoons oregano

2 tablespoons paprika

1/2 teaspoon thyme

1 tablespoon garlic powder

2 tablespoons salt

Mix all ingredients thoroughly.

COCKTAIL SAUCE

This is another simple sauce to prepare at home. You can prepare extra and store in the refrigerator.

Makes 1½ cups

1 cup ketchup

2 tablespoons lemon juice

1 tablespoon horseradish

1 teaspoon Tabasco sauce

Salt & pepper to taste

Whisk all ingredients together.

ROUX

Roux is a thickener for many sauces that's made by combining equal parts fat and flour. I like to use butter as the fat when I prepare a roux.

Makes 1 cup

1 stick (4 ounces) butter

1/2 cup flour

Start by melting the butter in a saucepan, and then slowly add the flour, whisking constantly. The roux is ready when the flour begins to lose its smell and the color darkens a bit, which takes about 2 to 3 minutes. Remove from the heat and cool. Roux can be refrigerated for up to one month.

MARINARA SAUCE

This is a very versatile and simple sauce to prepare. It can be eaten with plain pasta or paired with fish and vegetables. To prepare a tasty marinara, the key is to use the freshest ingredients, and be wary of overcooking the sauce. I like to prepare a large batch and leave leftovers in the fridge for an evening rendezvous with a piece of bread.

Makes 8 cups

   1/2 cup extra virgin olive oil

   5 cloves garlic

   11 cups canned tomatoes

   2 tablespoons powdered garlic

   2 tablespoons dry oregano

   2 tablespoons dry basil or 8 leaves of fresh basil

   2 tablespoons parsley, chopped

   1 tablespoon black pepper

   1½ tablespoons salt

Heat oil in a pan and sauté garlic until golden brown. Add tomatoes and spices, and begin to crush tomatoes with a whisk. Let sauce come to a boil, lower to a simmer and cook for approximately 30 minutes. Continue to whisk tomatoes while cooking until crushed. Remove from fire and cool.

PESTO SAUCE

The word pesto in Italian literally means 'to grind.' Pesto can be used in pasta recipes or can be used to flavor sauces, soups or meats.

I have basil growing throughout my garden so I can prepare extra pesto and freeze some for those long winter months.

I purée my pesto in the blender and top it with oil before refrigerating. The oil protects the pesto and adds to its shelf life.

Serves 6

2 cups basil

3 tablespoons pine nuts (or walnuts)

2 cloves garlic

1/2 cup extra virgin olive oil

Salt to taste

Process basil, pine nuts and garlic in the blender. Slowly drizzle olive oil until pesto thickens.

Tip: Add pesto to soups for extra flavor, use as a spread for sandwiches and bruschetta or as a topping for pizza. Put pesto into ice cube trays and freeze, then pop out and place in freezer bags.

VODKA SAUCE

I add prosciutto and bacon to our vodka sauce, giving it a smoky and sweet flavor. If you prefer a lighter vodka sauce, omit the meat.

This sauce is traditionally used for pasta but is also delicious on top of fried or grilled chicken.

Remember to remove the pan from the heat before deglazing with vodka.

Serves 2-4; enough for 1 pound of pasta

- 1 tablespoon prosciutto, diced
- 1 tablespoon bacon, diced
- 1 tablespoon butter
- 1/2 onion, minced
- 1 tablespoon vodka
- 12 ounces marinara sauce
- 1/4 cup heavy cream
- 1 tablespoon parsley
- 1 tablespoon grated cheese

Render bacon and prosciutto in pan with butter. Add onion and cook until wilted. Remove from heat and add vodka. Return to stove and burn off vodka.

Add marinara, heavy cream and parsley. Let sauce come to a simmer, reducing slightly, and cook for 2 minutes. Remove from heat. Toss in pasta and cheese and serve.

Serving Suggestions: Serve with pasta, fried chicken or pizza.

MEAT SAUCE

I like to mix together pork and beef to prepare my meat sauce. I grind up the meat together and sauté it with onions, carrots and celery. I then add it to marinara sauce and let it simmer for about 30 minutes.

Makes 10 cups

1/4 cup oil

1 small onion, minced

1 small carrot, minced

1 stalk of celery, minced

2 garlic cloves, minced

1/2 cup white wine

4 bay leaves

8 ounces ground pork

8 ounces ground beef

11 cups **marinara sauce**

Salt & pepper to taste

Sauté onions, carrots, and celery in oil until golden. Add garlic, brown. Deglaze with white wine. Add bay leaves and chopped meat. Cook together for approximately 10 minutes. Add marinara sauce; slowly simmer for about 30 minutes

MAYONNAISE

If you have ever prepared your own mayonnaise, then you know how difficult it is from then on to buy jarred mayo from the market. I love to lather mayo on a roast beef sandwich or place a light dab on a juicy burger. The mustard acts as an emulsifier and binds the oil and lemon with the yolk.

Makes 2 cups

2 egg yolks

1-2 tablespoons lemon juice (this supplies the acid)

1 teaspoon salt

2 teaspoons mustard

1-1½ cup oil

Whisk together yolks, 1/2 of the lemon, salt, and mustard until well incorporated. Slowly add the rest of lemon. Whisk in oil drop by drop until emulsion begins. Add the rest slowly.

VARIATIONS

Shallot Mayo Add shallots (minced) to provide a bit of sweetness and texture.

Aioli Add 1 garlic clove (minced). If serving with fish add capers.

Roasted Red Pepper Aioli We prepare this aioli to serve with crab cakes and other fried seafood dishes. You'll love the color.

PASTA, RICE AND POLENTA

Pasta is an essential part of a meal for Italians.

They either begin the meal with a bowl of soup or a bowl of pasta asciutta (which means 'dry').

Here in the states, we sometimes eat these dishes as a main course.

This first dish in Italy is called il primo piatto, and can also consist of risotto and polenta. The portion size is generally small, so as to leave room for il secondo.

For those days when you want to eat a simpler meal, il primo piatto can be served as a light main course.

FRESH PASTA

I learned how to make fresh pasta with my Grandma Anna in the basement of her home.

She had a special wooden board that she would place on top of her washing machine and we would make all different types of pasta, from gnocchi to fettuccine to maltagliati.

Grandma Anna would use the rolling pin on occasion to roll out the pasta, but she became accustomed to the convenience and speed of using a pasta machine.

Makes about 1 pound; serves 3-4

2 cups flour

3 eggs

Pinch of salt

1 tablespoon extra virgin olive oil

On a flat surface, make a well (see photo) with the flour. Add eggs, salt and oil. Begin to scramble the eggs and pull in the flour slowly. Have flour handy to dust hands if they get too sticky. Begin to knead the dough by hand. After a couple of minutes the dough will become elastic and smooth.

Cover the dough with plastic wrap and let it rest for 30 minutes. Pass it though the pasta machine until you reach your desired thickness. Cut with machine or by hand.

To cook, place in boiling, salted water for 2-3 minutes. Top with favorite sauce; eat immediately.

This recipe can easily be doubled or tripled.

LASAGNA

To prepare this recipe, you can either purchase the fresh pasta sheets or follow my Grandma Anna's recipe on the previous page. My wife Julia and daughter Gabriella were both fortunate to spend time with Grandma Anna drinking espresso at her home and learning how to make this delicious lasagna.

Serves 6-8

   1 pound fresh pasta

   1 quart (4 cups) meat sauce

   1 cup parmigiano, grated

   1 pound mozzarella, grated

Preheat oven to 350 F. Cook pasta al dente in salted boiling water, and drain.

Add 1/2 cup of sauce to bottom of 9x12 baking dish (2½ inches deep). Add one layer of pasta, spread meat sauce, sprinkle parmigiano, and mozzarella. Repeat the layers of pasta, sauce, parmigiano and mozzarella until the baking dish is almost full. For the last layer, I add only sauce and parmigiano.

Cover with tinfoil and place in oven for 1½ hours or until internal temperature is 160°F. Remove and let sit for 20 minutes before cutting.

HOMEMADE GNOCCHI

Gnocchi was the first pasta that my grandmother taught me to make. It was very popular in her region of Italy (Abruzzi) because potatoes could be harvested in the fall and stored all though the winter. Her homemade gnocchi, for me, was a real treat.

The key to a perfect gnocchi is to combine the flour and potatoes and then knead the ingredients *gently* until they come together. If the mixture is over-kneaded, the gnocchi will lose their delicate and light texture.

Serves 4

1 cup flour

1 egg

Pinch of salt

1 pound potatoes, cooked, mashed and cooled

Preferred sauce for serving such as marinara, cream sauce or meat sauce

Parmigiano cheese to taste

Form a well with the flour. Crack an egg in the middle of the well and mix. Add salt and mashed potatoes, mix gently. Knead until mixture comes together. Form into log and cut into pieces. Roll pieces into long strips and cut into 1½-inch pieces.

When cooking, drop gnocchi into boiling, salted water. Once they float to the top, remove them with a strainer. Add to sauce, such as marinara, cream sauce or meat sauce. Toss with parmigiano cheese. Serve immediately.

This recipe can easily be doubled or tripled.

POLENTA

Polenta was a very important food for my family back in Italy.

During long harsh winters, my grandma would have cornmeal stored in her cantina, along with wine and sausage, to see them through until spring. She would drizzle the cornmeal into boiling water and stir constantly with a wooden spoon so that the polenta would not stick to the pot. This whole process could take up to 30 minutes, but would produce a creamy, smooth polenta.

The problem was that you would be exhausted before you even sat down to eat.

I have discovered an easier way to prepare polenta, and my grandma agreed that my polenta was just as good, with a lot less effort.

Makes 4 cups

3 tablespoons salt

2 quarts water

1¼ cups cornmeal

2 ounces butter

Preheat oven to 350°F. Add 3 tablespoons salt to 2 quarts of water and bring to a boil. Drizzle the cornmeal slowly into boiling, salted water while whisking; this will eliminate any lumps that may form. Once the polenta has thickened, add the butter and give it one last whisk. Turn off the heat, cover it and place it in a 350°F oven for 30 minutes. Remove from the oven and serve.

You can also pour the cooked polenta into a sheet pan and level with a spatula. Let it cool. Polenta can be refrigerated for up to 4 days. Wrap tightly in plastic.

To reheat Cut polenta into any shape and bake, grill or sauté. At the restaurant, we reheat polenta by placing it underneath the broiler. Once the polenta begins to color, flip it over and cook the other side until golden. Top the polenta with your sauce.

Serving Suggestions: Serve with meat sauce, pesto, mushroom sauce or caponata.

If desired, add 1/2 cup grated parmigiano cheese.

Substitution Use chicken stock instead of water for a more flavorful polenta.

POLENTA BOSCAIOLA

One of my favorite pastimes with my dad was going to pick mushrooms at Cranberry Lake. We would wait for those damp days in the fall and head off with a sharp knife and a few prayers. My dad knew exactly which mushrooms were safe to consume, and we would both get excited, like kids in a candy store, when we found some hidden under leaves or tucked underneath a fallen log. Those mushrooms tasted delicious served with polenta.

Enough for 4 cups of polenta

1/4 cup olive oil
2 cloves of garlic, sliced

1 cup oyster mushrooms
1 cup shitake mushrooms
1 cup button mushrooms

Salt & pepper to taste
1 tablespoon butter
1/2 cup **marinara**

Sauté garlic in olive oil until golden. Add mushrooms, salt & pepper and toss, add butter. Sauté until mushrooms have released water and have released their flavor also. Add marinara and cook briefly until sauce has thickened. Ladle on top of polenta.

RICE

It seems as if rice is prevalent in most cultures; Italy is no exception. I love the versatility of rice. It can either be a main course or a simple accompaniment to any meal.

There are countless varieties of rice, such as long grain, white, brown, jasmine, and arborio, just to name a few. I prefer brown rice because it is healthier. The bran of the rice has not been removed, allowing for the rice to retain its nutrients. Arborio rice is short-grain rice that needs to be stirred continually for about 25 minutes to achieve a creamy consistency.

Here is the basic recipe for rice:

Serves 3-4

 1 cup rice

 2 cup water or chicken stock (2½ cups for brown rice)

 2 teaspoons salt

Combine all ingredients and bring to boil. Lower heat and simmer for approximately 20 minutes, making sure to stir every few minutes. Brown rice can take up to 40 or more minutes.

TIP: Leave rice a bit undercooked if you are going to reheat it later.

RICE PILAF & BEANS

This was the very first recipe that I taught the postulants at St. Joseph Friary. It is a fairly simple recipe to prepare and at the time their pantry was overflowing with beans and rice.

Serves 3-4

2 teaspoons olive oil

4 teaspoons onions, minced

1 cup rice

1 cup cooked beans, drained

2 tablespoons carrots, diced

2 tablespoons peas

2 cups chicken stock

1 teaspoon butter

2 teaspoons parmigiano cheese

Salt & pepper to taste

Sauté onions in oil until wilted. Add rice and coat with the oil. Add beans, carrots, peas and stock; bring to a boil.

Simmer uncovered for 20 minutes or until rice is al dente. Liquid should be completely evaporated. Take off heat, add butter and grated cheese. Mix and serve.

Risotto is a short-grain rice and takes longer to cook than long-grain rice. When prepared properly, it will produce a creamy, rich dish.

I like to sauté onions in olive oil and then add the risotto to coat. Then I add half of the water or stock and bring to a boil. The trick to risotto is to continuously stir it, and when the risotto gets dry, continue to add stock and stir. This will yield the creamy individual grains that give risotto its delectable appearance.

Serves 4-6

2 tablespoons oil

4 tablespoons onions, minced

3 cups Arborio rice

3 cups hot liquid*

1 tablespoon salt

Add pepper to taste

2 tablespoons parmigiano cheese (omit if making Risotto Pescatore)

2 tablespoons butter

1 tablespoon parsley

Sauté onions in oil until wilted. Add Arborio rice and toss to coat. Add hot liquid and bring to a boil. Lower heat to a simmer and continue to stir rice, adding salt & pepper. Add more liquid if rice is dry and under-cooked. When al dente, take off heat and mix in grated cheese, parsley and butter.

Tip: To save time, pre-cook the risotto. Add stock to cold risotto to reheat. Once heated, add ingredients and complete recipe.

*Use fish stock if preparing seafood risotto; use chicken stock when preparing risotto with meat.

RISOTTO BROCCOLI RABE & PROSCIUTTO

This is another example where it is ideal to combine broccoli rabe with sausage (in this recipe, I use prosciutto) and I add sundried tomatoes for color and flavor.

If you would like to prepare this as a vegetarian entrée, simply omit the prosciutto and use vegetable stock.

Serves 6-8

2 tablespoons oil	6 cups chicken stock, hot	2 tablespoons grated cheese
1 small onion, diced	1 pound broccoli rabe, parboiled and chopped	2 tablespoons butter
2 cups Arborio rice	2 tablespoons prosciutto, diced	1/8 teaspoon salt
		Pepper to taste

Heat oil in pot, add onions, sauté until soft. Add rice, stir for 1 minute to coat rice. Ladle 1 cup stock and simmer until absorbed. Continue slowly adding broth and simmering until rice is tender, about 18 minutes. Add broccoli rabe and prosciutto; stir together until well coated.

Remove from heat, stir in cheese, butter, salt and pepper.

Tip: To save time, cook risotto ahead of time. Add stock to cold risotto to reheat. Once heated, add vegetables, butter and cheese.

GRILLED VEGETABLE RISOTTO

This is a perfect dish during the summer months when the barbecue grill is on and you are grilling meat. Risotto is a perfect side dish to a juicy steak.

Serves 4-6

2 small zucchini, sliced

1 medium eggplant, peeled and sliced

2 portabella mushrooms

1/2 cup oil

1 small onion, diced

2 cups Arborio rice

6 cups chicken stock

1/4 cup grated cheese

2 tablespoons butter

Salt & pepper to taste

Prepare vegetables. In a large bowl, combine vegetables with 1/4 cup of the oil and salt, toss until well coated. Grill vegetables until both sides are browned and tender. Remove and slice portabella into strips. Heat the remaining 1/4 cup of the oil in pot; add onions, sauté until soft. Add rice; stir for 1 minute to coat rice. Ladle 1 cup of stock and simmer until absorbed, stirring constantly. Continue slowly adding broth and simmering until rice is tender, about 18 minutes. Lightly toss in grilled vegetables. Add cheese, butter, salt & pepper; stir until combined.

Serve immediately.

Substitutions Use any other vegetables in season. Add beans to this recipe to make it a heartier dish. Use canned beans if you don't have time to soak them overnight.

Tip: To save time, have risotto precooked. Add stock to cold risotto to reheat. Once heated, add vegetables, butter and cheese.

SHRIMP & ASPARAGUS RISOTTO

FamilyFoodandtheFriars.com

Spring is right around the corner when you begin to see beautiful bunches of asparagus in the produce aisle. I love to add shrimp to rice dishes, and they make a colorful presentation with the small spears of asparagus. In this recipe, you can either grill the asparagus or gently steam it for 3 to 4 minutes, keeping it crisp.

Serves 4-6

1 pound asparagus, trimmed & cut into 1/2-inch pieces
2 tablespoons oil

1 small onion, minced
2 cups Arborio rice
6 cups chicken stock, hot
10 medium shrimp, grilled

1/4 cup parmigiano cheese
2 tablespoons butter
Salt & pepper to taste

Grill or lightly steam asparagus. Heat oil in pot; add onion, sauté until soft. Add rice; stir for 1 minute to coat rice. Ladle 1 cup stock and simmer until absorbed. Continue slowly adding broth and simmering until rice is tender, about 18 minutes, constantly stirring. Add shrimp and cooked asparagus. Stir together until well coated. Remove from heat. Stir in 1/4 cup parmigiano cheese, butter, salt & pepper.
Serve immediately.
Substitution For more flavorful risotto add 1/4 cup diced prosciutto with the onions.
Tip: To save time, precook your risotto. Add stock to cold risotto to reheat. Once heated, add vegetables, butter and cheese.

ORECCHETTE BROCCOLI RABE & SAUSAGE

My Nonna Barile, aptly named because of the town in Italy where she lives, would always make this type of pasta by hand. My brother and I called them 'Army Helmets' because the pasta resembles helmets worn by British soldiers during WWII. The shape of these hats complements this recipe because the dimple in the pasta catches and holds the sauce.

Serves 4

1 bunch broccoli rabe, chopped

1/4 cup oil

2 garlic cloves, sliced

2 links sausage (4 ounces), casings removed

1/4 cup white wine

1 tablespoon parsley

1/8 teaspoon pepper

Pinch of red pepper flakes (optional)

1/2 cup chicken stock

1 teaspoon butter

1 pound orecchiette

Salt to taste

Parboil **broccoli rabe**

Heat oil in large sauté pan. Add garlic and sausage, cook until both garlic and sausage have browned. Toss in broccoli rabe. Deglaze pan with white wine; reduce wine and add spices and stock. Cook 5 more minutes, then remove from heat. Add butter, let melt.

Meanwhile, cook orecchiette in salted boiling water for approximately 10 minutes. Remove from water and strain. Toss pasta with sauce.

Serve over pasta or as a side dish.

Optional: Substitute sausage with sundried tomatoes or shrimp.

SPAGHETTI FRUTTI DI MARE

Translated 'Fruit of the Sea,' this dish is a great combination of shrimp, scallops and calamari. Avoid overcooking scallops, or else they will shrink and the meat will toughen. I prefer sea scallops over bay scallops. The sea scallops are larger and tend to have more flavor.

Serves 4-6

1 pound pasta

1/4 cup olive oil

2 cloves garlic, sliced

8 large shrimp, peeled and butterflied

2 cups (about 12 ounces) scallops, cup in half

2 tablespoons white wine

2 cups (about 8 ounces) calamari, cooked

2 tablespoons parsley

1 tablespoon basil

1 cup marinara

1/2 cup clam juice

Salt & pepper to taste

Heat oil in sauté pan; add garlic, sauté until golden. Add shrimp and scallops, stir and sauté for about 30 seconds, then deglaze with white wine. Sauté for another 30 seconds or until the wine has reduced. Add calamari, spices, marinara and clam juice. Cook for about 3 minutes or until scallops and shrimp are opaque.

In a large pot of boiling salted water, add pasta. Cook for 5-7 minutes, stirring occasionally, until pasta is al dente. Drain pasta, toss with sauce, and serve.

Substitution Can be served with risotto instead of pasta.

PIZZA & PANINI

At the restaurant, we bake our focaccia and focacciette fresh every day and use it for sandwiches or top it with cheese to serve like a pizza.

The difference between the focaccia and pizza is that we allow the focaccia dough to proof, that is, to grow, and when it is cooked, the crust becomes thicker.

It resembles bread and the thickness allows us to slice it in half and stuff for sandwiches.

PIZZA

My dad taught me how to make pizza at his restaurant in Yonkers when I was a little boy. His first experience with making pizza was using a coal oven in a pizzeria in Brooklyn, NY. The oven gave the pizza a distinctive smoky flavor and the pizzas were all cooked well done.

Over the years the coal ovens have died out, and we now use gas ovens. Gas ovens allow for the pizzas to cook evenly and are much easier to use. At the restaurant, we make our dough in 50-pound increments, cut the dough into 20-ounce portions, roll the dough into a ball and then refrigerate the dough to allow it to rise slowly.

One of our favorite pastimes during a snowstorm is to make dough with the kids and let them shape the dough into pizza. We get some pretty unique shapes, but the dough tastes great and the activity keeps the kids busy.

Serves 4

1 package dry yeast

1/4 cup warm water

3¼ cup flour

1½ teaspoons salt

3 tablespoons olive oil

1 cup cold water

Preheat oven to 450°F.

Dissolve yeast in warm water. Add the rest of ingredients together in a mixer and process for about 10 minutes or knead by hand. Shape dough into a ball and place into lightly oiled bowl. Let the dough rise until it has doubled in size, about 3 hours. The dough is now ready to be stretched.

If you are not going to be using the dough, cover and refrigerate immediately after kneading it. Make sure to cover it with plastic wrap so it will not dry out. Dough can be left in the refrigerator for up to two days.

Stretch dough into circle or rectangle, place on stone or cookie sheet. Top with sauce, mozzarella cheese and herbs. Place in oven until browned, about 15 minutes.

PIZZA MARGHERITA

In 1885, Chef Raffaele Esposito created the pizza margherita to honor the Queen of Italy, Margherita of Savoy. Thus was born the pizza margherita, a thin crust pizza topped with crushed tomatoes, fresh mozzarella and fresh basil leaves, the colors representing the Italian flag.

The trick to a tasty margherita pizza is to add spices to the crushed tomatoes and to layer the pizza with the basil leaves a minute before the pizza is finished cooking. Basil is a delicate herb that loses it flavor as it cooks.

Serves 4

20-ounce ball of dough

1 teaspoon oregano

1 teaspoon salt

1/2 teaspoon pepper

1 teaspoon garlic powder

3/4 cup crushed tomatoes

1 cup fresh mozzarella, cut in thin slices

8 basil leaves, chopped

Preheat oven to 400°F.

Stretch dough into circle or rectangle, place on stone or cookie sheet. Add spices to crushed tomatoes and mix. Add fresh mozzarella. Cook for approximately 15 minutes. Add basil; cook an additional minute. Remove from oven and allow it to sit for a couple of minutes before slicing.

PUTTANESCA PIZZA

This sauce is used primarily on pasta and fish, but we love to use it on pizza as well.

Serves 4

2 tablespoons oil

2 garlic cloves, minced

4 anchovies, chopped

1/2 cup kalamata olives, chopped

1 tablespoon capers

1 teaspoon salt

1/4 teaspoon pepper

1 cup marinara

6 leaves of basil

A pinch of red pepper flakes

20-ounce ball of dough

2 cups mozzarella cheese, shredded

Preheat oven to 400°F.

Heat oil in sauté pan; add garlic and sauté until golden. Add anchovies, olives, capers, red pepper flakes, salt & pepper. Let anchovies cook for a few seconds, then add marinara sauce and basil. Cook for only a minute to let the flavors blend together.

Stretch dough into circle or rectangle and place on stone or cookie sheet. Ladle on Puttanesca sauce, and sprinkle on cheese. Cook for approximately 15 minutes. Remove from oven and allow it to sit for a couple of minutes before slicing.

Suggestions: Add puttanesca to pasta, broiled or grilled fish.

PIZZA AL PESTO

Summer has arrived when the smell of basil is in the air. Pesto is famous for accompanying pasta, but it fares just as well perched on top of pizza.

Serves 4

20-ounce ball of **pizza dough**

1/2 cup **pesto**

2 tablespoons parmigiano cheese, grated, plus extra for sprinkling

1/2 cup shredded mozzarella

1 tablespoon olive oil

Preheat oven to 400°F.

Start by stretching the dough into the desired shape onto a cookie tray or pizza stone. Spread the pesto over the dough, leaving a border all around the edge. Sprinkle the cheese over the pesto and top with mozzarella and olive oil.

Bake for about 15 to 20 minutes or until edges have turned golden. Remove, sprinkle with a dusting of parmigiano cheese and serve.

ZUCCHINI PIZZA

This pizza has become one of our favorites at the restaurant. The key is to thinly slice the zucchini and to use a good quality extra virgin olive oil. I prefer to cook this pizza crispy and to add a few drops of oil before serving.

My daughter Sofia is by far the pickiest eater in the family. She despises zucchini but somehow this is her favorite pizza.

Serves 4

20-ounce ball of **dough**

1/4 cup extra virgin olive oil

2 cups zucchini, julienned

1 tablespoon salt

2 cups shredded mozzarella

Preheat oven to 400°F.

At the restaurant, we stretch the pizza dough into a thin crust and bake it in a rectangular sheet tray. It is very important to roll out the dough evenly to obtain a thin crust.

Once the dough is rolled out, place it on a sheet tray or pizza stone and drizzle olive oil over it, using a brush to spread out over entire dough. Spread the zucchini, sprinkle with salt and mozzarella cheese and drizzle a few more drops of oil.

Place the pizza in oven for 20-25 minutes or until the edges have turned golden brown.

Substitution If zucchini are not available, use portabella mushrooms.

CALZONE

Our calzones are also a popular item. We shape the calzone (which means 'trouser leg' in Italian) into a semicircle, and fill it with ricotta and mozzarella. It receives an egg wash before its journey into the oven.

Calzones can be stuffed with almost any ingredient, but a few of my favorites include spinach, prosciutto and mushrooms. My dad used to deep-fry his calzones, but we bake them in the oven for a healthier calzone. Don't forget the marinara sauce on the side for dipping.

Makes 4 large calzones

4 seven-ounce balls of **pizza dough**

2 cups ricotta

1/4 cup parmigiano cheese

1 cup mozzarella, diced

1 tablespoon parsley

1/2 teaspoon salt

1 egg

1/4 teaspoon pepper

Egg wash (1 egg yolk, beaten)

Preheat oven to 425°F.

In a large bowl, mix all the ingredients (except the egg wash) until well incorporated. Shape calzone by stretching the dough into a circle. Spoon the filling onto half of the dough, leaving a ½-inch border to allow room to seal calzone. Fold the other half of the dough over, pinching and pressing the edges together firmly to seal. Finish by either pushing the tong of a fork over the border to leave a decorative pattern or use a pizza cutter to trim a small piece of the border off.

Cut a small hole on top of the calzone to allow steam to escape.

Brush calzone with egg wash, place on a baking sheet and bake for about 15 minutes, until the calzone is golden brown.

FOCACCIA SANDWICH

The focaccia sandwich is one of our most popular lunch items at the restaurant. The bread is baked fresh daily and can be filled with a countless combination of ingredients. My family's favorite is the grilled chicken focaccia; I love to prepare them whenever we head out on a road trip or even if we are just having a picnic in the backyard.

Serves 4

4 seven-ounce balls of **pizza dough**

2 tablespoons olive oil

1/8 teaspoon sea salt

1/8 teaspoon oregano

1/8 teaspoon rosemary

2 tablespoons **balsamic dressing**

1/2 cup fresh mozzarella, sliced

1/2 cup **roasted peppers**

3 tomatoes, sliced

1 cup mesclun salad

4 grilled chicken breasts

Preheat oven to 425°F.

Shape focaccietta by rolling the dough with a rolling pin into a 6-inch circle. Place it on a pizza screen and brush focaccietta with olive oil; sprinkle with sea salt, oregano and rosemary. Let it sit at room temperature for about 1 hour, allowing the dough to double in size.

Bake for 20-25 minutes, or until golden brown. Transfer to a rack to cool.

Once focaccia has cooled, split focaccia in half lengthwise and spread on balsamic dressing. Add sliced fresh mozzarella, roasted peppers, tomatoes and mesclun salad. Add sliced grilled chicken. Cut each focaccia in half and enjoy.

Substitutions Replace chicken with prosciutto, grilled vegetables or cold cuts.

BRUSCHETTA

In my opinion, bruschetta has had a transformation in this country. My mom used to tell me stories about how they made bruschetta in their hometown. They would toast sliced bread over the fireplace to the point of burning it. (The word bruschetta means 'toasted'.) They would remove the bread from the fire and scrape off the charred bits, then take a piece of garlic and rub it across the bread. Finally, the bread would be drizzled with extra virgin olive oil and a pinch of salt.

At the restaurant, we have several variations of bruschetta. We top it with chopped tomatoes, kalamata olive spread, fresh mozzarella and even corn salsa. Be sure to use a firm bread, such as terranova or ciabbata, so the bread will not fall apart when the toppings are added.

BRUSCHETTA WITH FRESH TOMATOES

Serves 3

5 plum tomatoes, diced

5 basil leaves

2 tablespoons olive oil

1 clove garlic, minced

1 tablespoon fresh parsley, chopped

Salt & pepper

1/4 cup fresh mozzarella, diced (optional)

6 slices of bread

Mix all ingredients except bread in bowl. Let it sit for 1 hour to marinate. Toast bread, divide mixture among slices of toast.

BRUSCHETTA WITH BLACK BEAN SALSA

Serves 3

3/4 cup onions, diced

3/4 cup roasted peppers

1/2 cup tomatoes, diced

1 cup black beans

2 tablespoons cilantro, chopped

1 tablespoon lime juice

1 tablespoon olive oil

1 clove garlic, minced

6 slices of bread

Combine all ingredients except bread in bowl. Let sit for 1 hour. Toast or grill bread; divide mixture among slices of toast.

BRUSCHETTA WITH CORN SALSA

Serves 3

2 ears of corn, grilled

5 plum tomatoes, diced

1/4 cup red onion, diced

1/4 cup olive oil

1 tablespoon garlic, minced

1 tablespoon cilantro

2 tablespoons lime juice

Salt & pepper

1 jalapeño, diced (optional)

6 slices of bread

Grill corn, let cool. Cut corn off of cob, combine all ingredients except bread together. Let sit for 1 hour to marinate. Toast or grill bread; divide mixture among slices of toast.

BRUSCHETTA WITH BROCCOLI RABE & SAUSAGE

This is a hearty bruschetta that should be prepared in the fall or winter months.

Serves 3

2 tablespoons olive oil

2 cloves garlic, sliced

2 links sausage, casings removed

2 tablespoons chicken stock

1 bunch broccoli rabe, parboiled and chopped

6 slices of bread

Salt & pepper

Heat oil in sauté pan and sauté garlic until golden. Add sausage, crumble and cook until crispy, stirring occasionally. Deglaze pan with chicken stock, add broccoli rabe. Reduce heat and cook sausage through. Toast or grill bread, divide mixture among slices of toast.

Optional: Add sliced mozzarella on top of bruschetta and place under broiler to melt.

SOUPS

Soups are considered a primo piatto in Italy.

Most soups prepared in Italy tend to be hearty and can be served as a main course.

They range from minestrina, a thin soup, to minestrone, a thick vegetable soup that usually contains beans and pasta.

It is very important to use a flavorful stock when preparing your soup.

PASTA E' FAGIOLI

Serves 6 to 8

1/4 cup oil

1/2 cup onions, diced

2 cloves garlic, sliced

4 cups cannellini beans, canned or cooked

2 cups chicken stock

2 cups marinara

2 tablespoons parsley

Salt & pepper to taste

3 tablespoons butter

1/2 cup ditalini pasta

Parmigiano cheese to taste

Sauté onions in oil until wilted, add sliced garlic and sauté until golden. Add beans, stock, marinara, parley, salt & pepper. Let it come to a boil. Take soup off heat, add butter and let it melt.

Cook pasta al dente, drain and add to bean mixture. Sprinkle with grated cheese and serve.

Substitutions: Replace pasta with chopped escarole, spinach or kale.

Suggestions: Bean soup can be made ahead of time and reheated. Add more stock if it's too thick.

LENTIL SOUP

It seemed that my mom would always serve this soup to my brother and me when she wanted to punish us. It took me a long time to acquire a taste for lentil soup, but fortunately I did. Now every time I eat a bowl of minestra di lenticchia I think of mom.

Serves 8-10

- 2 tablespoons olive oil
- 1 small onion, diced
- 2 cloves garlic, sliced
- 1 celery stalk, diced
- 1 carrot, diced
- 1 pound lentils
- 7 cups chicken stock
- 1 small potato, diced

Heat olive oil in saucepan with onion until softened. Add garlic and sauté until golden. Add celery, carrot, and lentils, sauté until softened. Add stock and potato; bring to boil. Simmer for about 45 minutes or until potato and lentils are soft. Remove from heat and serve. Sprinkle parmigiano cheese to add flavor.

Optional: Add tiny cubed pieces of salami while sautéing vegetables to add a smoky flavor.

Split Pea Soup

Serves 8-10

- 2 tablespoons olive oil
- 1 onion, diced
- 2 garlic cloves, sliced
- 1 pound split peas
- 1 celery stalk, diced
- 1 carrot, diced
- 1 bay leaf
- 8 cups water
- 1 ham hock
- Salt & pepper

Heat oil in saucepan, add onion, cook until wilted. Add garlic and vegetables, cook until garlic is golden. Add ham hock and water; bring to a boil for approximately 1 hour.

Reduce heat to a simmer and cook until split peas are tender. Take out ham hock and remove meat from bone. Chop meat into small cubes and add to soup.

Ham hocks can be bought raw or fresh as well as smoked or cured. They are ideal for using in soups and stews.

Suggestions: If you do not have a ham hock, dice 3 slices of ham and add while soup is cooking.

MINESTRONE

At my restaurant, we strive for a colorful and lively minestrone. This soup appears to have many ingredients, but the effort in preparing it is well worth it.

Serves 8-10

1/2 cup olive oil

1 medium onion, diced

2 garlic cloves, sliced

2 small carrots, diced

2 celery stalks, diced

1 potato, peeled & diced

1 cup frozen peas

1 cup string beans

1/2 cup white cabbage, cored & diced (or spinach)

7 cups chicken stock

1/2 cup great northern beans, canned or cooked

1/2 cup chickpeas, canned or cooked

1 cup **marinara**

2 tablespoons salt

2 tablespoons garlic powder

Sauté onion in oil until soft. Add garlic; cook until golden. Add vegetables, stock, marinara, salt and garlic powder. Bring to a boil, simmer for approximately 1 hour, or until vegetables are soft. Add beans and allow soup to come back to a boil.

STRACCIATELLA SOUP

This is a wonderfully simple soup to prepare. The key to a tasty stracciatella soup is to use fresh eggs and plenty of parmigiano cheese. My dad used to add hot cherry peppers to this soup to give it a kick. The word stracciato in Italian means 'little rag,' which refers to the appearance of the egg and cheese once it is cooked in the soup.

Serves 3-4

4 cups chicken stock

1 egg, lightly beaten

1 cup packed shredded spinach

Salt & pepper to taste

1/4 cup parmigiano cheese

Lightly beat egg while bringing broth to a low simmer. Whisk the egg into soup, add spinach, salt & pepper. Cook on low heat for about one minute. Remove from heat and serve hot. Fold in parmigiano cheese.

Suggestions: To make a heartier soup, add mini meatballs

Substitution: Use escarole in place of spinach or any other leafy greens.

POTATO & LEEK SOUP WITH PANCETTA

I love to prepare this soup during cold winter months. It is a hearty soup, yet it has a smooth texture with complex flavors.

Serves 4-6

1 bunch leeks, washed & diced

1/2 cup pancetta, diced

2 tablespoons butter

3 potatoes, peeled & diced

2 bay leaves

3 cups chicken stock

1/2 cup heavy cream

Salt & pepper to taste

1/4 cup parmigiano cheese

1 teaspoon nutmeg

1 tablespoon chives, chopped

Trim top of leek. Sauté pancetta and butter in saucepot. Render fat from pancetta and add leeks; sauté until soft, about 2 minutes. Add potatoes and bay leaves; stir. Add stock and bring to a boil, simmer for approximately 30 minutes or until potatoes are soft. Add cream, salt, pepper, parmigiano and nutmeg. Return to boil and remove from heat. Purée soup in a blender*; add chives and serve.

Tip: To prevent the liquid from spattering, allow the heat to escape: Remove the cap from the hole in the lid, and cover the lid with a dishtowel when blending.

*Hot liquids will expand when blended, so be careful not to fill the jar of the blender more than halfway (purée in batches if necessary).

CREAM OF ASPARAGUS SOUP

Serves 6-8

  3 pounds asparagus

  3 tablespoons butter

  1 onion, diced

  1 teaspoon salt

  Pepper to taste

  8 cups chicken stock

  3/4 cup heavy cream

Prepare the asparagus by gently snapping off the end of each spear. Cut the remaining spears into ½-inch pieces. In a large pot, add butter and onions; let onions cook until soft. Stir in asparagus, salt and pepper, cook for 1 minute. Add stock, bring to a boil, return to a simmer for about 15 minutes or until asparagus is very tender.

Pour soup into blender* and purée until smooth. Return to pan. Stir in heavy cream. Check for consistency. If soup is too thin, add more cream; add more stock if soup is too thick. Bring soup to a boil for a few seconds. Remove from heat. Serve hot.

Tip: To prevent the liquid from spattering, allow the heat to escape: Remove the cap from the hole in the lid, and cover the lid with a dishtowel when blending.

*Hot liquids will expand when blended, so be careful not to fill the jar of the blender more than halfway (purée in batches if necessary).

I borrowed this recipe from my wife because it is simple yet delicious. Our kids love to have an evening snack of tomato soup and grilled cheese. The secret is to use vine-ripened tomatoes or a quality canned tomato, such as Italian San Marzano tomatoes.

Serves 6-8

2 tablespoons oil or butter

1/2 onion, diced

Two 28-ounce cans of diced tomatoes or 8 cups of fresh plum tomatoes, diced

2 cup chicken stock

2 tablespoons fresh basil, chopped

2 tablespoons fresh parsley, chopped

1 teaspoon salt

Pepper to taste

2 tablespoons cream (optional)

Heat oil in a soup pot; add onions and sauté until soft. Add tomatoes, stock and spices. Let it come to a boil, reduce heat and let simmer for about 20 minutes, stirring occasionally. Whisk in cream and cook 1 more minute. Remove from heat. For a smooth, creamy soup, carefully purée in blender*. Serve hot.

Tip: To prevent the liquid from spattering, allow the heat to escape: Remove the cap from the hole in the lid, and cover the lid with a dishtowel when blending.

*Hot liquids will expand when blended, so be careful not to fill the jar of the blender more than halfway (purée in batches if necessary).

CHICKEN BARLEY SOUP

This soup yields a large quantity of soup. It can be eaten as a snack or as a main course. It reheats well, so I always like to have it left over. I recommend cooking this soup during those long, cold winter months when you need something to fill you up and keep you warm.

Soak the barley in water overnight to make it more tender and to quicken the cooking time.

Serves plenty (makes about 1 gallon)

- 4 tablespoons oil
- 1 large onion, diced
- 1 garlic clove, chopped
- 1 tablespoon butter
- 2 celery stalks, diced
- 2 carrots, diced
- 1 pound barley
- 1 cup button mushrooms, sliced
- 1 pound chicken breast, skinless & boneless, cut into 1-inch cubes
- 1 cup marinara
- 20 cups (5 quarts) chicken stock
- 1/2 cup peas
- 2 cups spinach
- 1½ tablespoons salt
- 1/2 teaspoon pepper

Heat oil in large pot and sauté onion until soft. Add garlic and cook until golden. Add butter to melt. Add remaining ingredients and bring to a boil. Reduce to a simmer and cook for approximately 45 minutes or until the barley and vegetables have become tender. Serve hot.

PUMPKIN BISQUE

I know autumn has arrived when I start cooking Pumpkin Bisque at the restaurant. You will rarely find this on an Italian menu, but that doesn't stop me from preparing this delightful soup.

Serves 6-8

- 1/4 cup butter
- 1 small onion, diced
- 1 celery stalk, diced
- 1½ pounds pumpkin, peeled and cut into ½ cubes
- 2 tablespoons parsley
- 1/4 teaspoon cinnamon
- Salt & pepper to taste
- 4 cups chicken stock
- ½ cup heavy cream
- A pinch of nutmeg
- 1 tablespoon ginger, peeled & grated
- 1 tablespoon honey

In a stockpot, melt butter, add onions and celery, then sauté until soft. Add pumpkin, parsley, cinnamon, salt & pepper, stir to coat. Add stock and simmer until pumpkin is tender, about 20 minutes. Add cream to thicken and let soup return to a slow boil. Remove from heat and add honey, nutmeg and ginger. Carefully purée in blender* for a smooth, creamy soup. Serve hot.

Tip: To prevent the liquid from spattering, allow the heat to escape: Remove the cap from the hole in the lid, and cover the lid with a dishtowel when blending.

*Hot liquids will expand when blended, so be careful not to fill the jar of the blender more than halfway (purée in batches if necessary).

MEAT, CHICKEN & FISH

Il secondo piatto, or main course, quickly follows il primo.

When my dad was living in Italy, meat was scarce and they would have to wait until Sunday to slaughter a rabbit or chicken.

He grew up eating his share of lentils and chickpeas, and there was never a discussion of high cholesterol in his household.

Italians tend to keep main dishes small, and serve them with grains and vegetables on the side.

During the warmer months, the second course is prepared simply, usually grilled or sautéed.

But in the winter months, braising, roasting and cooking stews are more common.

At the restaurant, our customers love to combine the second course with their first course; for instance, a succulent veal chop served with a side of ziti in the same sauce.

TENDERIZING MEAT: CHICKEN AND VEAL

Using a mallet to tenderize meat allows you to shape and stretch it to the desired thickness and size. Place meat between two large pieces of plastic wrap to create less splatter.

I like to use top round for my veal scaloppine recipes because it is a tender cut. Try to cut pieces into medallion sizes and cut the top round against the grain. If scaloppine is cut along the length of the grain, it will shrink and toughen when cooked.

Use a mallet to stretch the meat out and do not pound down directly on the meat.

The same principle holds true for chicken. I slice the chicken breast lengthwise in half before using the mallet, thinning it out evenly. A thin chicken breast will cook evenly and will stay moist.

GINO'S BREADCRUMBS

Breadcrumbs are used to coat chicken, veal, fish or any vegetable that you are going to fry. I add olive oil to my breadcrumbs only if I am going to use with fish. They make a perfect topping to broiled filet of sole or baked stuffed clams. Store breadcrumbs in an air-tight container in refrigerator.

3 cups breadcrumbs

1½ teaspoons paprika

1 tablespoon oregano

1 tablespoons garlic powder

1/4 teaspoon black pepper

1 teaspoon salt

2 tablespoons parsley

2 tablespoons parmigiano cheese

1/2 cup oil (optional)

Mix all ingredients in large bowl.

Suggestions: Use breadcrumbs with zucchini, zucchini flowers, shrimp, or fish.

MEATBALLS

I learned how to make meatballs from my dad when I was 8 years old. His secret was to add extra grated cheese to impart more flavor. He used to tell me when he was a boy growing up in Italy, the mixture consisted mainly of breadcrumbs and milk, with the addition of very little meat.

My mom and dad would spend Sunday mornings rolling mini meatballs with my oldest two children, Gabriella and Michael.

Makes about 25 meatballs

4 pounds chopped meat

2 cups **bread crumbs**

3 tablespoons salt

2 tablespoons garlic

1 tablespoon black pepper

2 tablespoons oregano

1 cup parmigiano cheese

4 eggs

1 cup milk

2 tablespoons parsley, chopped

Preheat oven to 400°F.

Combine all ingredients and mix well. Mixture should be firm but not too hard. Use an ice cream scooper to shape the meatballs and then finish pressing and rolling them by hand.

Bake in oven for 30 minutes. Meatballs are ready when the internal temperature reaches 160°F.

Tip: To taste mixture, boil water and drop 1 tablespoon meat mixture into water to cook.

CHILI

This is yet another recipe 'borrowed' from my wife. She loves to sneak vegetables in her chili to make it healthier and more colorful for the kids. It also adds another layer of texture to the recipe, and can be served as a complete meal.

Serves 6-8

2 pounds chopped meat

1/2 cup olive oil

1 large onion, diced

3 garlic cloves, sliced

2 carrots, diced

1 zucchini, diced

1 jalapeño, diced (optional)

1 tablespoon garlic powder

1½ tablespoons salt

1 teaspoons pepper or to taste

1 tablespoon chili powder or to taste

1 tablespoon oregano

2 teaspoons cumin

1/2 teaspoon red chili pepper or to taste

1 tablespoon cilantro, chopped

56 ounces diced tomatoes (2 large cans)

15 ounces black beans, canned or cooked

15 ounces kidney bean, canned or cooked

Cook meat in sauté pan until brown. Drain and set aside.

Sauté onions in oil in large pot until tender. Add garlic, carrots and zucchini and jalapeño, stirring until golden. Add chopped meat and spices; stir. Add tomatoes; cover and simmer for about 45 minutes, stirring occasionally. Add beans; simmer another 20 minutes or until desired thickness.

Serving suggestion: Serve with rice or as taco or tortilla filling; top with sour cream, grated cheddar cheese and avocado.

BEEF STEW

When I was a young boy growing up, my mom would take us to Italy for the summer. My brother and I loved to spend time with our family there, and we would adapt quickly to Italian life. One morning, my grandfather brought me to his farm to pick almonds and chestnuts. During lunchtime, grandma delivered a pot of beef stew and roasted potatoes. I still remember the smell of that stew when she handed me the plate. I have tried to replicate that same wonderful meal, but I've added vegetables to introduce more color and texture.

Serves 6-8

- 1 large onion, diced
- 3 garlic cloves, sliced
- 2 tablespoons oil
- 1 large zucchini, diced
- 2 carrots, diced
- 3 small red potatoes, diced
- 2 pounds stew meat
- 1/2 cup red wine

- 1 tablespoon oregano
- 4 bay leaves
- 1 tablespoon rosemary
- 1 tablespoon garlic powder
- 28-ounce can plum tomatoes
- 1 cup frozen peas
- 2 tablespoons butter (optional)
- Salt & pepper to taste

In a large pot, sauté onions and garlic in oil until soft. Stir in zucchini, carrots and potatoes, continue to sauté for about a minute. Add meat and cook until brown. Deglaze pan with red wine; add remaining ingredients, except peas. Let liquid reduce. Cover pot and let simmer for approximately 2-3 hours or until meat is tender. Add peas and 2 tablespoons of butter (optional) and cook another few minutes. Remove from heat and serve.

VEAL SCALOPPINI PIZZAIOLA

The top round is the most tender cut of veal. Cut the veal into 3-ounce medallions and tenderize the meat with a mallet. I use button mushrooms in this recipe, but feel free to substitute with any other variety of mushroom.

Serves 2

8 ounces veal scaloppini

1 cup flour

2 ounces olive oil

2 garlic cloves, minced

1/4 cup white wine

1 cup mushrooms, sliced

1 tablespoon parsley, chopped

Salt & pepper

1/2 cup chicken stock

3/4 cup **marinara** sauce

1 tablespoon butter

Tenderize the veal by pounding it with a mallet. Dip the veal into flour and place it into a hot pan with oil, browning veal quickly on both sides and removing from pan. Add garlic to brown. Deglaze the pan with wine, let the liquid reduce. Add mushrooms, parsley, salt & pepper, sauté until mushroom are tender. Add chicken stock and place veal back into sauté pan. Let stock reduce a bit and add marinara sauce. Once the sauce thickens, remove from heat and swirl in butter.

Serve with a side of grilled polenta or risotto.

CHICKEN ROLLATINI

When making chicken rollatini, it is very important to pound the chicken breast with a mallet until it is thin and even.

Serves 4-6

6 large chicken cutlets, thinly sliced

2 cups **breadcrumbs**

1/4 cup flour

2 eggs

Oil for frying

Ricotta Stuffing

2 cups ricotta

2 tablespoons parmigiano cheese

2 slices ham or prosciutto, diced

2 tablespoons sun dried tomatoes, sliced

1 cup cooked spinach

1/2 cup mozzarella, shredded

1 egg

1/4 teaspoon salt

A pinch of pepper

Sauce

4 tablespoons oil

2 tablespoons onion, diced

1 tablespoon parsley

1/4 cup white wine

2 tablespoons sun dried tomatoes

1 cup chicken stock

1/4 cup demi-glace *(or 1 teaspoon flour)

Salt & pepper

1 tablespoon butter

Preheat oven to 400°F.

Combine all stuffing ingredients in a bowl and mix thoroughly. Placing one-sixth of the mixture in the center of each cutlet, roll the cutlets like tortillas, folding both sides in tightly. They are traditionally breaded and fried in oil. Dip in flour, then into the beaten egg and roll in bread crumbs.

Heat oil in large sauté pan; fry chicken until browned on all sides. Place in baking dish. Place in oven for 8 to 10 minutes or until the internal temperature is at least 150°F. Discard oil. Continue by preparing the sauce in the pan while baking the rollatini in the oven. In the same pan, add oil and onions, stir until brown. Deglaze hot pan with wine, stirring and scraping up bits, about 20 seconds. Add stock, spices, sun dried tomatoes and *demi-glace . Let sauce cook, stirring occasionally, for about 5 minutes or until sauce has thickened.

Add chicken back to pan to coat with sauce. Turn off heat and add butter, swirling until melted. Cut the rollatini in half, transfer chicken to serving dish and pour on sauce for a beautiful presentation. Serve hot.

*When substituting flour for demi glace, sprinkle flour after deglazing pan with wine.

Tip: For a healthier alternative, lightly batter the rollatini in flour and sauté in olive oil.

CHICKEN PARMIGIANO

Chicken Parmigiano is hands-down my customers' favorite entree. The key to an excellent chicken parm (as our customers call it) is tender chicken, tasty sauce and a copious amount of grated cheese. It is very important to pound the chicken breast thin and even with a mallet.

My son Michael began working at the restaurant at the age of eight, helping his grandma Ivana seat customers and work the register. He would arrive famished, work 30 minutes and then ask 'Is it time to eat?'

His meal of choice would always be Chicken Parmigiano.

Serves 4-6

6 chicken cutlets, thinly sliced

1 cup flour in a bowl

1 egg, beaten, in a bowl

2 cups **breadcrumbs**, in large bowl

1 cup canola oil for frying

1/2 cup **marinara** sauce

3 tablespoons parmigiano cheese

1/2 cup mozzarella cheese

Preheat oven to 400°F.

Begin by dipping both sides of the chicken cutlet in the flour. Dredge in egg, shaking off excess egg, and then place in breadcrumbs, pressing the breadcrumbs firmly into the chicken with the palm of your hand.

Pour about 1 inch of oil into a large sauté pan. Heat on medium; when oil is hot, add chicken and sauté until both sides are golden brown. Remove and place on a paper towel to soak up any excess oil.

In a large baking dish, add a ladle of sauce. Place breaded chicken in the dish, add sauce to the top of the chicken. Sprinkle with parmigiano and fresh mozzarella.

Bake for approximately 20 minutes or until the cheese has melted and has begun to brown.

Substitutions Grilled chicken for a wheat-free alternative. Use vegetables such as eggplant or zucchini.

POLLO ESTIVO

My wife came home from lunch one day and declared excitedly, "I just had this fried chicken topped with lettuce, tomatoes and mozzarella." I quickly retorted, "Jul, we also have that dish. It's called Pollo Estivo." The look on her face was priceless. This dish is ideal to serve in the summer with a nice glass of Pinot Grigio.

Serves 4

2 tablespoons olive oil

4 thinly sliced chicken cutlets, **breaded**

1 cup tomatoes, diced

1 teaspoon parsley, chopped

1/4 cup fresh mozzarella, diced

1/4 teaspoon oregano

1/8 teaspoon salt

1/8 teaspoon black pepper

1 cup mesclun salad, chopped

Heat oil in large frying pan; slowly add chicken cutlets. Meanwhile, in large bowl, lightly toss all remaining ingredients together, with the exception of mesclun. Once the chicken is browned and cooked through on both sides, remove from pan and place on paper towel to drain excess oil. Place chicken on serving dish, top each chicken breast with mesclun salad and then add tossed mixture.

Serve and enjoy.

ROASTED CHICKEN WITH
SEA SALT & ROSEMARY

FamilyFoodandtheFriars.com

This recipe is ideal when you are looking to whip up a quick and easy meal. My wife prefers to roast the chicken at a high temperature to allow the skin to become crispy. The result is a beautifully colored and tasty meal. My kids and I end up fighting over the skin.

Serves 4-6

1 whole chicken

1 -1½ teaspoons sea salt

1 cup water or chicken stock

1 stalk of fresh rosemary

Pepper to taste

Preheat oven to 475°F.

Remove giblets from inside chicken. To butterfly chicken: cut through the side of the back bone of the chicken. Open chicken and place in a cast iron skillet or baking dish so all the meat is facing up.

Sprinkle with sea salt, add water or stock, rosemary and pepper to bottom of pan. Place in preheated oven for about 1 hour or until juices run clear and the skin of the chicken is crispy and golden brown. Remove from pan and let sit. Scrape dripping, pour in sauté pan or leave in cast iron skillet, add 1/2 cup of water. Let simmer on stove to reduce liquid, add salt and pepper if needed. Carve chicken, place on serving dish, pour reduced liquid over top and serve.

Substitutions Use sage, thyme or parsley instead of rosemary.

Suggestions: Reserve bones after carving and use for a chicken stock.

QUICHÉ

This is a relatively quick and simple recipe. It is an inexpensive meal, but is so versatile and the kids love it (and so do I).

Serves 4

2 tablespoons butter or olive oil

1 cup each vegetable, chopped

Salt & pepper to taste

12 fresh eggs

1 cup cheese, grated or chopped

1/4 cup heavy cream (optional)

POSSIBLE VEGETABLE & CHEESE PAIRINGS

Use 2 cups vegetables and 1 cup plus 2 tablespoons cheese

asparagus & brie

broccoli, onion & cheddar

tomato, onion & mozzarella

bacon, onion & cheddar

zucchini, onions, parmigiano & cheddar

spinach & parmigiano

mushroom & cheddar

Preheat oven to 350°F.

Butter 10-inch pie pan. In a sauté pan, heat oil or 1 tablespoon butter. Add chopped vegetables, sprinkle on salt & pepper, sauté until tender. Remove from heat.

In a mixer or with a whisk, beat eggs until fluffy, about 3-4 minutes. By hand, mix in 1 cup cheese and cooked vegetables. Ladle into buttered pie pan. Top with 2 tablespoons cheese, salt & pepper. Place into oven, cook for about 25 minutes, or until middle is set. Remove from oven and serve.

OSSO BUCO

FamilyFoodandtheFriars.com

Italians are well known for not wasting anything, and Osso Buco is a perfect example of their frugality. Veal shank is a very tough cut of meat, but braising it for 3-4 hours allows the meat to become so tender that it begins to fall off the bone.

Make sure to cover the osso buco once in the oven, and with a fork, try to pull the meat away from the bone. Once the meat can be easily separated from the bone, you are now in luck. Enjoy.

Serves 4

1/2 cup olive oil for sautéing

4 veal shanks

1/2 cup flour

1 small onion, diced

1 small carrot, diced

1 celery stalk, diced

½ cup red wine

2 cups marinara sauce

1 cup chicken stock

1 tablespoon parsley, chopped

Salt & pepper to taste

In a bowl mix together and set aside:

Gremolata (a garnish consisting of minced parsley, lemon and anchovy)

1 anchovy, chopped

lemon peel from 1/2 lemon

1 tablespoon parsley

Preheat oven to 350°F.

Heat oil in a large sauté pan. Roll the veal shanks in flour and sauté all sides until brown. Remove from pan. Add onions, carrots and celery; sauté until vegetables are golden. Deglaze pan with wine and reduce. Add marinara sauce, stock, parsley, salt & pepper, bring to boil and add veal shank. Place in baking dish, and into a 350°F oven. Cook until meat reaches desired tenderness, around 3 hours. You will see the meat begin to fall off the bone. Remove from oven, place sauce in pan. Add gremolata to sauce and mix well. Let sauce come to a boil; remove from heat. Pour sauce over veal in serving dish.

Suggestions: Risotto is an excellent side dish with Osso Buco. Polenta also works well.

LEG OF LAMB WITH GARLIC

My mom was born in L'Aquila, a little town in the Abruzzi region of Italy. It is famous for its cuisine, most notably for its cheese and sausage. Whenever we were in Italy during Easter time, mom would go to the farm and order a baby lamb to be 'prepared' for dinner. The lamb was so succulent and tender, and yet so simple to cook. Here is her recipe:

Serves 12

2 cloves garlic, sliced

Leg of lamb 6-8 pounds

2 tablespoons parmigiano

4 tablespoons parsley, chopped

2 tablespoons oil

Salt & pepper to taste

2 medium onions, chopped

1 tablespoon flour or butter

1 tablespoon tomato paste

2 cups chicken stock or water

2 tablespoons rosemary, chopped

Preheat oven to 400°F.

Peel garlic and cut lengthwise into thin slices. Puncture meat, making small pockets, around 10-12 in total. Add cheese, garlic and parsley into each slit. Rub meat with olive oil and sprinkle rosemary, salt & pepper. Place in oven for 20 minutes. Lower oven to 350°F and add chopped onions. Baste roast and cook for one more hour, removing from oven when internal temperature reaches 135°F.

Remove roast from pan. Place pan over low heat and sprinkle flour over the juice, or swirl in butter. Cook for one minute. Add tomato paste, and cook another minute. Add stock slowly, allowing to thicken. Simmer for 20 minutes. Pass through fine mesh strainer and pour sauce over roast.

CALAMARI MARINARA

FamilyFoodandtheFriars.com

Calamari (squid) is a favorite at the restaurant. There are two ways to cook calamari: hot and quick or slowly simmered. Fried calamari are tender because they are cooked very quickly in hot oil. The antithesis is our calamari marinara, which is slowly simmered in a pot. We cook our calamari for about 45 minutes, and the end result is a tender, soft and tasty squid.

Calamari comes in different sizes. I recommend 5-8, which denotes the length of the tube in inches. You can buy calamari frozen in a package with the tentacles separated from the bodies. You can also buy them fresh, but they tend to be cumbersome to clean and you create a huge mess in the process. There is not much difference in taste between the frozen and fresh.

Serves 8-10

2 tablespoons olive oil

2 cloves garlic, sliced

5 pounds calamari

2 tablespoons white wine

1 cup marinara

To prepare calamari

In a pot of water, add 1-inch cut calamari (enough water just to cover calamari). Let water come to a boil, reduce heat to a simmer. Let calamari simmer for about 45 minutes or until calamari can be picked up and torn apart easily. Drain calamari and use in any recipe.

Heat oil in large sauté pan with garlic. Add calamari. When garlic is lightly browned, deglaze pan with white wine. Let wine reduce. Add marinara sauce just until heated.

Suggestions: Serve with pasta or rice.

FILET OF SOLE

There are countless varieties of sole, but the authentic filet of sole is called Dover sole. It has a firm, sweet, and lean flesh. Unfortunately, it is very expensive and is usually served only at upscale restaurants. The filet of sole that most people purchase in the store is technically not sole, but is in fact flounder.

When buying flounder, look for smooth, firm, white flesh and make sure that the store fillets it for you. Due to its leanness, flounder is perfect for steaming or baking. Our most popular method of cooking sole is to broil it and top it with bread crumbs.

Serves 2-3

1 teaspoon butter
4 filets, around 4 ounces each
4 tablespoons white wine
2 tablespoons lemon juice

1 tablespoons parsley, chopped
1 teaspoon capers
4 tablespoons fish stock or clam juice
Salt & pepper to taste

3 tablespoons bread crumbs
2 teaspoon olive oil
Pinch of paprika
Preheat oven to 400°F.

Prepare a baking dish by rubbing the bottom with butter. Place sole in baking dish by folding each end under the middle. Add white wine, lemon, parsley, capers, stock, salt & pepper. Top fish with bread crumbs, sprinkle paprika and drizzle oil over bread crumbs to prevent burning. Place in oven for about 10 minutes. The fish is cooked when you are able to pierce the flesh of the fish and the fish flakes apart easily.

SWORDFISH MOJO

Swordfish is a versatile fish that has a meaty firm texture which allows it to be grilled, roasted, boiled or sautéed. Make sure that you cut swordfish steaks around 1¼ inches thick, or else you run the risk of overcooking the fish and losing its moistness.

Serves 4

4 pieces swordfish, cut into 1/4 inch thick steaks

1/4 teaspoon salt

1/8 teaspoon pepper

1/4 cup olive oil

1 tablespoon onion, minced

1 clove garlic, minced

2 tablespoons white wine

1½ cup orange juice

1/4 cup demi-glace (optional)

1 tablespoons cilantro, chopped

1/2 teaspoon sugar

1 tablespoon butter

Heat grill. Season swordfish with salt and pepper, then brush with olive oil. Place fish on hot grill, cook for about 3 minutes per side or until fish is opaque in the center.

Meanwhile, in a large sauté pan, heat oil. Sauté onion until soft, add garlic until golden. Deglaze pan with white wine and cook for about 20 seconds. Add lemon juice, demi-glace, cilantro and sugar. Cook until sauce has reduced by half, around 3 minutes. Remove from heat. Add butter and allow to melt.

Top fish with the hot sauce.

ALMOND SALMON

One day my brother was preparing trout almondine and asked how almonds would taste on salmon. I told him to try it and the rest was history. This is probably our most sought-after dish in the restaurant. The almonds add a sweet texture to the salmon and help the fish retain its moistness.

I recommend waiting to add salt to this dish until after it is cooked.

Serves 2

2 pieces of 8-ounce salmon

1 cup flour for dredging

1 egg (for batter)

1/4 cup almond slices

1/4 cup oil

1/4 cup white wine

3/4 cup clam juice

1½ tablespoons lemon juice

1/4 cup demi-glace (optional)

1 tablespoon parsley, chopped

1/8 teaspoon pepper

Pinch of salt

1 teaspoon flour (optional)

1 tablespoon butter

Preheat oven to 400°F.

Dip salmon filet into flour, then in egg batter and finally press filet into almonds with the skin side up. Heat oil in large sauté pan. Add salmon with almonds, face down into oil. Turn salmon over after 20 seconds so as not to burn the almonds. Finish sautéing on other side for about 30 seconds. Remove fish from pan, place in baking dish and put in 400°F oven for 8 minutes to finish cooking.

Meanwhile, discard oil from pan and deglaze with wine. Reduce wine by half and add remaining ingredients, with exception of butter. When sauce has reduced by half, remove from heat and add butter. Melt butter and taste, add salt as desired.

Place salmon on serving dish, top with sauce.

Suggestions: Serve salmon over a bed of sautéed spinach.

SHRIMP SCAMPI

When buying shrimp, size does matter. Shrimp are sold by how many pieces are in one pound. For instance, u-15(under 15) denotes that there are approximately 15 shrimp per pound.

I prefer to work with jumbo or extra large because they create a more appealing presentation on the plate and there is too much work involved in cleaning the smaller shrimp. For this recipe, use extra-large shrimp, peeled and deveined, but leave the tail on for a more attractive presentation.

Serves 3 to 4

1/4 cup olive oil
1 clove garlic, minced
15 shrimp, peeled and deveined
2 tablespoons white wine
1½ tablespoons fresh lemon juice

3/4 cup clam juice
1 tablespoon parsley, chopped
Pinch of pepper
1 tablespoon butter
Salt to taste

Heat oil in sauté pan with garlic. Once the garlic begins to sizzle, add shrimp. When the garlic begins to brown, deglaze the pan with white wine. Add lemon, clam juice, parsley and pepper. Cook until shrimp are opaque, about 3 minutes. Take off heat; add butter, stirring to melt. Taste sauce; add salt if needed.

Place shrimp on serving dish, pour sauce over shrimp and serve.

Tip: The key to preparing succulent shrimp is not to overcook them or the shrimp will toughen and dry out. Cooking time for shrimp is only a couple of minutes.

Tip: Always add butter to a sauce after you remove the pan from the heat. The excessive heat will cause the butter to separate from the sauce and will give your sauce an oily appearance. Gently swirling the butter will reduce this separation.

MUSSELS MARINARA

Mussels are a very popular shellfish in Italian cooking. They possess a sweet yet firm texture and can be prepared in countless ways. To prepare mussels for cooking, sort through them and discard any shells that are broken or open. Rub the mussels together vigorously for a minute to remove any sand or barnacles. Do not let the mussels soak in water for an extended period of time. Pull off any barnacles with a knife and twist off any beards (the hairlike tufts protruding from the shells). Keep mussels refrigerated until ready to cook.

Serves 2

3 tablespoons olive oil	20 mussels	1 tablespoons parsley, chopped
2 cloves garlic, minced	1/4 cup white wine	
	1 cup **marinara**	

Heat oil in sauté pan, add garlic and cook until golden. Add mussels, wine and parsley. Sauté for 30 seconds and then add marinara. Cover and cook mussels until they open. Remove from pan and serve.
Suggestions: Pairs well with pasta, rice, or risotto.

VEGETABLES

Vegetables are an integral part of an Italian's diet.

They are served on the side of il secondo piatto and also can be served as an appetizer.

It is important to eat vegetables when they are in season.

The cost will always be less and the vegetable's flavor will be enhanced.

ASPARAGUS

To grill Grilling is an excellent cooking technique that allows the natural sugars in vegetables to caramelize, releasing the deep rich sweet flavors. To prepare, trim bottom of spear by gently snapping off by hand or cutting with a knife. Toss asparagus with **balsamic dressing** or olive oil, salt & pepper. Let sit for 15 minutes. Place on hot grill and let cook for about 5 minutes, turning occasionally.

To roast To prepare, trim bottom of spear by gently snapping off by hand or cutting with a knife. Toss asparagus with **balsamic dressing** or olive oil, salt & pepper. Let sit for 15 minutes. Place asparagus in baking dish and place in a 400°F oven for about 10 minutes, or until tender, turning occasionally.

To steam Place asparagus in a steamer basket over boiling water in a covered pan. I prefer steaming vegetables because they retain their flavor and nutritional value better than other cooking methods.

Suggestions: Serve with fish, pork, beef, lamb, eggs or as a topping for salad.

GRILLED EGGPLANT WITH SMOKED MOZZARELLA

When shopping for eggplant make sure to buy a firm, smooth and glossy-skinned fruit (believe it or not, eggplant is classified as a fruit). Keep eggplant refrigerated and try to use them quickly because they are very perishable and develop a bitter flavor as they age.

Serves 2-4

1 eggplant, peeled, cut into 1/4-inch slices

1/4 cup **balsamic dressing**

1 eight-ounce ball of smoked mozzarella, sliced

Marinate sliced eggplant in balsamic dressing for 15 minutes. Place on hot grill; cook about 2 minutes on each side. Top with smoked mozzarella, let melt and serve.

Substitutions Sprinkle grilled eggplant with parmigiano cheese and ladle marinara sauce on top. Layer with mozzarella and bake in a 400°F oven until cheese is melted, about 10 minutes.

FAMILY, FOOD AND THE FRIARS

PORTABELLA SALTIMBOCA

A portabella mushroom is a mature crimini mushroom that possesses a dense meaty flavor. In my opinion, it is as close to eating meat as you can get without actually consuming animal flesh. I love the flavor and boldness of portabella and they can be cooked in a variety of ways, such as grilling, sautéing and steaming.

Serves 2-4

To prepare mushrooms

Trim the stalks of 4 portabella mushrooms. Set aside and wipe the caps with a damp paper towel. Drizzle oil, salt and pepper over mushrooms and let sit for 20 minutes.

To make topping

1/4 cup olive oil	Salt & pepper to taste
2 cloves of garlic, sliced	4 portabella mushrooms
1 link of sausage, casing removed, chopped	4 slices mozzarella cheese
1/2 cup chicken stock	Preheat oven to 400°F.
4 ounces broccoli rabe, cooked & chopped	

Heat oil in sauté pan and add garlic. Add sausage and sauté. When garlic and sausage brown, deglaze pan with stock and add broccoli rabe, salt and pepper. Cook until stock has evaporated and sausage is cooked through.

Meanwhile, grill portabella mushroom on both sides until cooked. Add topping and place a slice of mozzarella cheese on top. Place on baking sheet and place in oven just until cheese has melted.

Substitutions: Use spinach or escarole in place of broccoli rabe.

ROASTED POTATOES

FamilyFoodandtheFriars.com

My dad would always talk about cultivating potatoes on his farm in Italy and bringing them home to roast in the wood oven. His ingredients were simple: extra virgin olive oil, fresh rosemary, salt, pepper and a dash of grated cheese. I still think of dad every time I eat roasted potatoes. You can use either Idaho or red potatoes.

Serves 6-8

3 pounds potatoes, washed, cut into 1-inch cubes

1 tablespoon fresh rosemary, chopped

1 teaspoon oregano

1/2 teaspoon salt

1 tablespoon parsley, chopped

4 tablespoons extra virgin olive oil

1 teaspoon parmigiano cheese

In a large bowl, toss cut potatoes with all ingredients except cheese. Pour onto a baking tray, place into oven for 45 minutes to an hour or until potatoes are golden brown, stirring every 15 minutes.

About 10 minutes before potatoes are cooked, sprinkle with cheese and toss well.

Suggestions: Serve with any roasted meats, chicken or fish.

MASHED POTATOES

Serves 8-10

4 pounds potatoes, peeled and cut into cubes

1 cup heavy cream

4 tablespoons butter

1 tablespoon salt

2 tablespoons chives

Pepper to taste

2 tablespoons grated cheese

Bring large pot of salted water to a boil. Add potatoes and simmer for about 20 minutes or until tender. Drain potatoes, pass through a food mill, or mash by hand and set aside. Meanwhile, in a sauce pan, heat cream and butter until melted and cream comes to a boil. Remove from heat, add cream mixture to potatoes, stirring in salt, chives, pepper and cheese. Taste to determine need for salt. Serve hot.

Tip: For creamier potatoes, add more cream.

CAPONATA

This recipe was given to me by my Zia Lucia, a wonderful aunt and cook. Caponata is a traditional Sicilian dish consisting of various ingredients. The flavors in Caponata are complex yet blend perfectly.

Makes 4 cups

5 medium-sized eggplants, peeled & diced

1 tablespoon salt

1½ cup olive oil

5 red bell peppers, cut into small cubes

5 small onions, diced

1 celery stalk, diced

1 cup tomatoes, peeled, seeded and diced

3 tablespoons capers

2 tablespoons sugar (optional)

2/3 cup red wine vinegar

2 cups kalamata olives, chopped

2/3 cup parsley, chopped

1 teaspoon oregano

Salt and pepper to taste

Place diced eggplant in colander, mix evenly with salt. Let eggplant drain its natural juices for about 1 hour; this helps remove its natural bitterness. Pat dry with paper towel. In a large frying pan, fry the eggplant in 1 cup of olive oil until soft, then remove. Add the diced peppers and fry until soft. Remove from pan. Discard oil. In the same pan, heat 1/4 cup oil. Add onions and celery, sauté until golden. Add tomatoes and simmer for 5 minutes. Stir in capers, sugar, vinegar, olives, parsley, oregano and remaining 1/4 cup olive oil. Let simmer for 5 minutes, stirring occasionally, allowing the flavors to marinate. Remove from pan. Toss all ingredients together in a large bowl and allow to cool. Add salt and pepper to taste.

Tip: Caponata should be served at room temperature.

Optional: Bake eggplant and peppers in a 400°F oven for a healthier dish.

Suggestions: Serve as a side dish or as a spread for crostini.

ROASTED SWEET POTATOES

I cannot imagine eating Thanksgiving dinner and not serving sweet potatoes. They can be prepared countless ways. My favorite is to slice them and roast them in the oven, allowing them to caramelize and become sweet.

Serves 8-10

10 medium-sized sweet potatoes

1/4 cup olive oil

1 tablespoon honey

Salt & pepper to taste

Preheat oven to 425°F.

Peel and cut sweet potatoes into 2-inch long slices. Place in baking dish. Add remaining ingredients and toss well. Roast in oven for about 40-45 minutes, mixing occasionally, until sweet potatoes are soft and begin to brown.

SAUTÉED RED PEPPERS

Serves 6

2 tablespoons olive oil

5 red peppers, seeds removed and cut into 1-inch squares

1 tablespoon parsley, chopped

Salt to taste

In a large sauté pan heat oil. Add peppers, cover and let sauté for about 10 minutes, stirring occasionally. Add parsley and salt. Continue to sauté until peppers soften and begin to brown.

ROASTED PEPPERS

Roasting enhances the natural sweetness and the flavor of the vegetable. Red peppers are best when roasted, because they are ripe and are much easier to peel than green peppers.

Serves 4-6

6 red peppers

1 clove garlic, sliced

1/4 teaspoon oregano

1 tablespoon fresh basil, chopped

1 tablespoon parsley, chopped

1/4 cup extra virgin olive oil

1/2 teaspoon salt

1/8 teaspoon black pepper

Simply place the peppers on a baking sheet and place them under the broiler, charring each side completely. Remove from oven, place peppers in a bowl and cover to allow them to steam for about 15 minutes. This steaming will make them easier to peel. Peel and discard skin and seeds, placing the peppers into a bowl. Pull the peppers into strips, add remaining ingredients and toss. You are now ready to enjoy a taste of heaven.

Roasted peppers can be refrigerated for a few days. Bring them to room temperature before serving.

Suggestions: Perfect complement to fresh mozzarella, also ideal for sandwiches and salads.

An Italian cookbook would be incomplete without mentioning broccoli rabe. Also known as cima di rabe, these bitter greens are a favorite in my house and should be eaten during the fall and winter months.

Remove the bitterness from the rabe by parboiling before sautéing.

Serves 4-6

- 2 pounds broccoli rabe
- 3 tablespoons olive oil
- 2 cloves garlic, sliced
- 1/2 teaspoon salt
- 1/8 teaspoon pepper
- 1 teaspoon butter
- 1½ tablespoons chicken stock

Snap off stems and remove outside leaf of the broccoli rabe stalk.

Parboil broccoli rabe by placing stem down into a pot of boiling, salted water. Cover and let boil for about 3-4 minutes or until the stems are tender. Drain broccoli rabe and blanch in cold water. Drain well.

In a sauté pan, heat oil and sauté garlic until browned. Add parboiled broccoli rabe, salt, pepper and butter. Add stock as juices reduce. Cook until broccoli rabe is tender.

Tip: Parboiled broccoli rabe can be refrigerated for several days before sautéing.

Serving suggestion: Broccoli rabe can be eaten as a side dish or can be served with pasta, chicken or sausage.

ARTICHOKES

The edible part of the artichoke plant is the green globe-like bud, picked either small or mature. The mature artichoke develops a tough fuzzy 'choke' that needs to be removed. When selecting artichokes, look for firm globes with tight, green leaves. The most popular way Italians prepare them is by stuffing them with breadcrumbs and braising them.

Serves 4

4 artichokes

4 tablespoons provolone, chopped

4 cups **breadcrumbs**

4 tablespoons olive oil

2-3 cups chicken stock

Begin by plucking off the outer leaves. Cut off 1 inch off the top of the artichoke. With a spoon, scoop in from the top and remove the choke (the center) from the inside of the artichoke. Cut and peel the stem to form a flat bottom. Reserve the stem. Cut the reserved stem into cubes and place them and 1 tablespoon of cut provolone into the center of each artichoke. Fill the center and between the leaves of the artichoke with breadcrumbs. Drizzle 1 tablespoon oil over each artichoke.

Place artichokes in roasting pan and add 1 inch chicken stock to bottom of pan. Cover with foil, let come to a boil. Reduce heat to a simmer and braise for about 45 minutes, making sure liquid does not evaporate. Add stock if needed. Artichokes are ready when their leaves are easily pulled off or when the heart can be pierced with a fork.

AVOCADO & BEAN SALAD

The first food that we introduce to all of our children when they are ready to eat solid foods is avocado. Avocados contain many nutrients and are high in monounsaturated fats, perfect for a growing child.

This salad contains many different colors and textures; it can even be used as a topping for bruschetta. My kids and I prefer to eat it simply with a spoon accompanied by a juicy steak.

Serves 8

2 avocados, diced

12 ounces kidney beans

12 ounces black beans

12 ounces garbanzo beans

2 mangos, peeled and diced

1 small onion, diced

1/4 cup fresh cilantro, chopped

1 apple, diced

Juice of 1 lemon

1/4 cup olive oil

Salt & pepper to taste

Mix all ingredients together and serve.

Serving suggestion: Great for a side dish to any meal.

FAVORITES AT GINO'S

When *Gino's Trattoria* in Mahopac, NY, first opened its doors in 1994, the menu featured mainly southern Italian cuisine.

Our menu has evolved to include an abundance of northern Italian recipes as well as a few Latin specialties.

We have the privilege to cook dinner for families, and it is my responsibility to listen to what they want to eat.

We have been blessed to have such incredible customers who are passionate about eating and who love to share recipes with us.

Some of our dishes are even named after them.

I could write an entire cookbook on our favorite recipes, so it was difficult to choose a few of the more popular dishes.

SAN FRANCISCO CIOPPINO

A cioppino is a fish stew made with tomatoes and several types of fish and shellfish. My brother debuted this dish a few years ago and it has been a hit ever since. Most people associate fennel with sausage, but we use it sparingly in this dish to transform the flavor. It adds a hint of fragrance and compliments the seafood. Be sure to wash the mussels and clams before cooking and have a couple of pieces of bread handy for dipping.

Serves 4 to 6

2 tablespoons olive oil

1 tablespoon onions, chopped

1 tablespoon carrot, minced

1 tablespoon garlic, minced

1/8 teaspoon fennel seed

1/4 white wine

4 pieces filet of sole

1 cup **calamari**, cooked

10 littleneck clams

20 mussels

8 extra-large shrimp, peeled, deveined and butterflied

1/2 cup marinara sauce

3/4 cup clam juice

Heat oil in pan and add onions and carrot. Sauté until soft and add garlic, cooking until golden. Add spices fennel seeds and deglaze pan with wine. Add seafood, sauce and clam juice. Cover and simmer for 5 minutes, until shellfish has opened and filet of sole is opaque. When fish is cooked, remove from pan and let sauce reduce for 1 minute. Place fish in plate and cover with sauce.

PORK LOIN ZANFARDINO

This dish was named in honor of a customer who was looking for something a bit different one evening. He was tired of ordering the same grilled pork chops, and asked if I would bread them, fry them and prepare them with potatoes and red peppers. It sounded like a great dish, with the breadcrumbs keeping the pork moist and tender, while soaking up the delicious sauce. It has been a great addition to our menu at the restaurant.

Serves 3-4

Breading (see below)

Eight 1-inch thick pieces of pork loin

1 cup vegetable oil for frying

2 tablespoons onion, diced

1 cup button mushrooms, sliced

2 tablespoons white wine

1 tablespoon fresh lemon juice

1 cup chicken stock

2 tablespoons parsley, chopped

Salt and pepper to taste

1 potato, peeled & sliced thin

2 tablespoons olive oil

1/2 cup **demi-glace**

2 tablespoons roasted peppers, chopped

Breading

1/2 flour in bowl

2 eggs, beaten in bowl

1 cup **breadcrumbs**

Begin by breading pork with flour, egg and breadcrumbs. In large frying pan, heat 1/2 cup oil and fry the breaded pork on both sides until golden. Remove from oil and place on top of a paper towel to drain excess oil. Discard frying oil.

Sauté onions in 2 tablespoons of oil until soft. Add mushrooms and sauté until golden. Deglaze the pan with white wine; add lemon, stock and spices.

Meanwhile, in a frying pan, heat ½ cup oil fry sliced potatoes in a pan. Once potatoes are tender, add to sauté pan with sauce. Add demi-glace and cooked pork to pan. Allow sauce to come to a boil and place in 400°F oven for 10 minutes. Internal temperature of pork should be at least 140°F.

Remove from oven and serve.

FETTUCCINE SEAFOOD

I rarely use milk or cream in any recipe that contains fish, but this dish is an exception. I add a touch of cream to the marinara sauce to give a beautiful color and to add richness to the sauce. The key is to only add a touch of cream so it will not overwhelm the delicate flavor of the seafood.

Serves 4-6

1/4 cup olive oil

2 cloves garlic, sliced

12 shrimp (extra large) peeled and deveined

2 cups (16 ounces) large scallops

1 tablespoon parsley

Pinch of salt & pepper

2 tablespoons white wine

1½ cups **marinara**

1/4 cup heavy cream

2 pounds fettuccine

Heat oil in large sauté pan. Add garlic, sauté until golden. Add shrimp, scallops and spices. Cook briefly, about 1 minute. Add white wine to deglaze pan. Cook wine for 30 seconds, stir in marinara and cream. Simmer sauce until thickens, about 2 minutes. Meanwhile, cook pasta.

Toss sauce with fettuccine and serve.

GNOCCHI, PROSCIUTTO AND PEAS

This sauce is ideal for using with homemade gnocchi. The fresh dumpling will soak up the sauce and the peas will add a pleasant color and texture to the dish. Cooking prosciutto causes it to lose its prized delicate texture, so I like to use the less expensive American prosciutto for this dish. Prosciutto di Parma should be reserved for eating uncooked and is usually served as an antipasto.

Serves 4-6

- 1 tablespoon butter
- 2 tablespoons prosciutto, diced
- 1 tablespoon parsley chopped
- Salt & pepper to taste
- 3 tablespoons peas
- 1 cup heavy cream
- 1 pound gnocchi
- 2 tablespoons parmigiano cheese

Melt butter in a large sauté pan. Add prosciutto; sauté until the fat is rendered and the prosciutto has turned color, around 1 minute. Add spices and peas, sauté briefly, add cream. Cook until cream reduces by half, about 2 minutes. Cook gnocchi, drain and toss with sauce and parmigiano cheese. Serve immediately.

BLACKENED SALMON POMEGRANATE

When we first cooked salmon with pomegranate sauce, I wasn't sure what to expect. Fortunately, I was pleasantly surprised by how the sweetness of the sauce and the spiciness of the salmon complement each other. Pomegranate juice is a bit tart, but when reduced in a sauce pan, becomes sweeter and fuller in flavor. If you are hesitant to use the blackened spice, use it sparingly, but be sure to try it with this sauce.

Serves 2

2 cups spinach, steamed

2 salmon filets, 6-8 ounces each

2 tablespoons Blackened Spice Rub

1/4 cup olive oil

1 tablespoon butter

1 teaspoon onion, diced

1 clove of garlic, chopped

1 tablespoon white wine

Pinch of salt & pepper

1 teaspoon parsley, chopped

1/2 teaspoon sugar (optional)

1/2 cup pomegranate juice

1/2 teaspoon fresh lemon juice

Preheat oven to 400°F.

Coat one side of salmon filet with Blackened Spice Rub. Heat oil in sauté pan. Add salmon spice side down. Cook for 20 seconds then flip salmon over, sautéing for another 30 seconds. Remove salmon from pan, place in baking dish, bake in oven for about 8 minutes. Discard oil from pan. Add 1 tablespoon butter and onion, sauté onions until they soften, about 1 minute. Add garlic and cook until golden. Deglaze pan with wine and reduce. Add spices, lemon juice and pomegranate juice. Let sauce reduce by half, about 5 minutes. Remove from heat and melt 1 tablespoon butter in sauce.

Place salmon on a bed of steamed spinach, ladle on sauce and serve.

Substitutions Use blackened shrimp or scallops and grill.

CHICKEN SCARPARIELLO

My father would add hot cherry peppers into every dish, including his lentil soup. These peppers add a spicy flavor, and give color and texture to any dish. If you are wary of the spiciness, remove the ribbing from inside the pepper along with the seeds to lessen the heat. We like to serve this dish with chicken breasts, but you can also use chicken on the bone.

Serves 3-4

6 chicken breasts

Flour for chicken

1/4 cup olive oil

2 cloves garlic, sliced

1/4 cup white wine

Juice of 1 lemon

1 cup chicken stock

1 teaspoon rosemary

1/8 teaspoon salt

1 tablespoon parsley, chopped

1/4 cup demi-glace or flour

2 tablespoons cherry peppers

Gently pound chicken into 1/4-inch thickness. Lightly flour chicken. In a large sauté pan, heat oil, then add chicken. When chicken starts to brown, turn over, cook through, about 3-4 minutes. Transfer chicken to plate.

Discard oil from pan. Add garlic to pan and brown. Deglaze hot pan with wine, stirring and scraping up bits, about 20 seconds. Add lemon, stock, spices, cherry peppers and demi-glace. Let sauce cook, stirring occasionally, for about 5 minutes or until sauce has thickened. Add chicken back to pan to coat with sauce. Turn off heat and add butter, swirling until melted. Transfer chicken to serving dish, pour on sauce. Serve hot.

Optional: If you do not have demi-glace, thicken sauce with 1/4 teaspoon of flour. Add flour after pan is deglazed with wine.

RISOTTO PESCATORE

Serves 4-6

To prepare risotto

4 tablespoons onions, minced

2 tablespoons oil

3 cups Arborio rice

3 cups hot liquid (use fish stock if preparing seafood risotto, use chicken stock when preparing risotto with meat)

1 tablespoon salt

2 tablespoons butter

1 tablespoon parsley

Sauté onions in oil until wilted. Add Arborio rice and toss to coat. Add hot liquid and bring to a boil. Lower heat to a simmer and continue to stir rice, adding salt & pepper. Add more liquid if rice is dry and undercooked. When al dente, take off heat and mix in butter and parsley.

To prepare pescatore

1 tablespoon garlic, minced

2 tablespoons olive oil

2 tablespoons white wine

10 mussels

6 bay scallops

6 pieces jumbo shrimp

1 tablespoon parsley

3/4 cup marinara sauce

Sauté minced garlic in olive oil. When garlic is browned, deglaze pan with wine, add fish and sauté for 1 minute. Add parsley and marinara sauce, cover and cook for about 3 minutes or until mussels have opened and seafood is cooked. Take off stove and toss with risotto.

THANKSGIVING FEAST

For Italians, Thanksgiving is not about the turkey.

Growing up, my family would begin with a huge antipasto, followed by soup and pasta, and then the turkey would be trotted out. Everyone was full by then and the turkey was left unscathed.

THANKSGIVING MENU

Turkey
Cranberry Sauce
Ham
String Beans
Sweet Potatoes
Mashed Potatoes
Penne Vodka
Stuffing
Apple Pie
Pumpkin Pie
Sticky Date Pudding Cake with Caramel Sauce

I never knew the taste of turkey until I got married and hosted out first Thanksgiving holiday. I was delighted and surprised by the flavor and juiciness of that crispy roasted turkey.

Thanksgiving became a very special holiday for my family when we began to travel down to the friary in Harlem and cook Thanksgiving dinner for the Franciscan Friars of the Renewal and their neighborhood. It is a great way for us to begin the holy season of Christmas.

We stick with the traditional menu, but I make sure not to forget to cook penne alla vodka for Fr. Luke.

Our first Thanksgiving feast with the friars took place in 2007, and consisted of five turkeys, one spiral ham, and all the various trimming that accompany the holiday. It has grown to 12 turkeys, two spiral hams and over 100 neighbors.

Dad (me) performs the cooking with the help of the friars and my children.

Once the food is ready, the children position themselves on the serving line and dinner is served (with the help of the brothers).

It has become a joyous and uplifting experience for my family to bring happiness to those who may be alone during the holiday

I prefer to cook a 12-14 pound fresh turkey for our thanksgiving meal. To prepare the turkey, remove the giblets (heart and gizzards) from the cavity of the turkey and lather the turkey with the rub. Apply the rub the night before cooking. The marinade will add moisture and will result in a more flavorful and tender turkey.

Serves 10-15

12-14 pound turkey

1/2 cup turkey rub

1 large onion, cut in quarters

2 carrots, chopped

4 celery stalks, chopped

1 cup chicken stock or water

Preheat oven to 350°F.

Place turkey in a large roasting pan. Surround with cut vegetables and stock. Place in oven. Make sure to baste the turkey every 20 minutes. A 12-pound turkey should take 3 to 3½ hours and the internal temperature should reach 160°F. When turkey is cooked, remove from pan and allow to rest for 20 minutes before carving.

To make gravy

Strain vegetables from roasting pan, pour drippings into a sauce pan. Add 1 cup stock or water into roasting pan, stirring and scraping to remove any brown bits. Add to saucepan. Allow saucepan with drippings to come to a boil. Add 1 tablespoon of flour, whisking continually, for 30 seconds. Lower heat to a simmer. Allow gravy to thicken for around 1 minute. Remove from heat and pour gravy through a strainer to remove any lumps.

Tip: For every pound of meat, you need 15 minutes of cooking time.

BAKED HAM

I love to serve ham as a complement to turkey on Thanksgiving. I purchase ham that is already pre-cooked and pre-sliced and just follow the directions for heating and serving. Place sliced pineapple on top of the ham before placing it in the oven. The pineapple will caramelized and release its sugar into the ham.

Serve with mustard.

STRING BEANS

Serves 12 -15

  2 pounds string beans

  1/2 cup olive oil

  4 cloves of garlic, sliced

  Salt & pepper to taste

To prepare string beans, wash and trim both ends. Add string beans to a large pot of boiling salted water. Allow them to cook for 3 to 5 minutes, or until tender. Remove from heat and strain.

In a sauté pan, heat oil and garlic. Let sauté until garlic is golden. Toss in string beans. Add salt & pepper to taste and serve.

CRANBERRY SAUCE

Makes about 2 cups

1 cup water

1 cup sugar

12 ounces dry cranberries

1/2 teaspoon orange zest

Bring water and sugar to a boil, stirring until sugar dissolves. Add cranberries; simmer until berries soften, about 10 minutes. Stir in zest. Pour in serving bowl, let cool. Serve.

STUFFING

FamilyFoodandtheFriars.com

Stuffing is the perfect complement to turkey and gravy.

Serves 10

2 sausage links, casing removed, chopped

1/2 cup butter

1 onion, diced

2 celery stalks, diced

1 apple, diced

2 cups chicken stock

1 tablespoon dried sage

1 teaspoon dried thyme

2 teaspoons rosemary, chopped

1 teaspoon salt or to taste

Pepper to taste

1/2 cup dried cranberries or raisins

8 cups bread, cubed

1 cup walnuts, chopped (optional)

Preheat oven to 400°F.

Place sausage in a large, deep skillet. Cook over medium-high heat, stirring until evenly brown. Remove the sausage from the skillet and let drain on paper towels. Combine butter with the sausage drippings until butter has melted.

Sauté onion, celery and apple in the butter mixture until onions are tender. Add chicken stock, sausage, spices, raisins, walnuts, salt & pepper. Place bread in a large bowl. Pour onion mixture onto the bread, tossing gently with your hands until well mixed. Pour into a large baking dish. Place in oven until crispy, about 25-30 minutes. Serve hot.

TURKEY RUB

This rub will add flavor as well and allow the skin to turn golden and crispy.

Makes 3/4 cup

1 clove garlic, minced

1/4 teaspoon rosemary, minced

2 teaspoon salt

1 teaspoon paprika

1/4 teaspoon thyme

1/2 teaspoon pepper

1/2 teaspoon oregano

1 tablespoon parsley

Juice of 1 lemon

1/2 cup olive oil

Prepare the rub by mixing all the ingredients thoroughly. Smear all over turkey and let sit refrigerated overnight.

DESSERTS

DESSERTS HAVE ALWAYS BEEN AN ESSENTIAL PART OF AN ITALIAN MEAL, BUT TYPICALLY THEY USE SIMPLE INGREDIENTS SUCH AS ALMONDS, CHOCOLATE, CHERRIES, CITRUS AND ANISE.

IF YOU HAVE JUST ENJOYED A TRUE ITALIAN MEAL, FROM ANTIPASTO TO IL SECONDI PIATTO, YOU MIGHT FIND IT DIFFICULT TO ENJOY A FILLING DESSERT.

SOME CUSTOMERS SKIP THEIR MEAL AND GO STRAIGHT TO DESSERT (I'M NOT RECOMMENDING THAT).

ITALIAN CHEESECAKE

There are two types of cheesecake that we prepare at the restaurant: American and Italian. American cheesecake contains cream cheese and is topped with sour cream. Italian cheesecake, on the other hand, contains ricotta. It is amazing the difference in flavor that the different types of cheeses give to these desserts. Don't forget to have a short cup of espresso to accompany your cheesecake.

Serves 12

1/2 cup butter

1 cup cookie crumbs for shell

3 pounds ricotta

6 eggs

2 cups sugar

1/4 cup anisette

1 teaspoon vanilla extract

1 teaspoon almond extract

1 teaspoon orange zest, grated

1 cup chocolate chips (optional)

Preheat oven to 375°F.

Lightly butter 9-inch springform pan. Melt butter, mix well with cookie crumbs, pour into pan, distributing evenly and pressing firmly to coat sides and bottom. In a large bowl, whisk or use mixer to blend remaining ingredients, pour into cookie crust. Bake for 1 to 1½ hours, until middle has set and top of the cake is golden. Remove from oven and let cool. Serve cheesecake at room temperature.

Tip: Toothpick inserted into the middle of the cheesecake should come out clean when it's ready.

CREME BRÛLÉE

We all keep trying to reinvent creme brûlée by adding flavors to the custard, such as raspberry or blueberry. There are just some things in life that can't be improved, no matter how creative we try to be, and creme brûlée falls into that category. Use fresh vanilla bean when executing this recipe.

Serves 8

4 cups heavy cream

1 vanilla bean, cut lengthwise and scrape out beans

1/8 teaspoon almond extract

1/2 cup sugar

6 egg yolks

Preheat oven to 350°F.

In a saucepan, add cream, vanilla beans and almond extract and bring to a boil. Take off heat immediately after the mixture has come to a boil.

Meanwhile, in a large bowl, whisk well sugar and egg yolks. Slowly pour hot cream into egg mixture, whisking constantly. Divide custard into 8 single-serving ramekins.

Place ramekins into a large baking dish; add water to the bottom of the baking dish 1/4 of the way up the ramekins. Bake for about 45 minutes or until middle has set. Remove from oven and let cool.

To serve, lightly coat the top of each ramekin with sugar and use a small torch or place them under the boiler to caramelize (fancy word for burn) for about 30 seconds. Serve.

PIE CRUST

Makes 2 pie crusts

 2 cups flour

 1 teaspoon salt

 2/3 cup plus 2 tablespoons cold, unsalted butter

 4-5 tablespoons cold water

 Dash of cinnamon (optional)

Mix flour, cinnamon and salt in medium bowl. Cut in butter, using pastry blender (or pulling two table knives through ingredients in opposite directions), until butter is the size of small peas. Sprinkle with cold water, 1 tablespoon at a time, tossing with fork until all flour is moistened and pastry almost leaves side of bowl (more water can be added if necessary).

Gather pastry into a ball, then divide in half. On a lightly floured surface, shape into two flattened disks. Wrap both pastry in plastic wrap and refrigerate about 45 minutes or until dough is firm and cold, yet pliable. If refrigerated longer, let pastry soften slightly before rolling.

Roll one pastry at a time on lightly floured surface, using floured rolling pin, into circles 2 inches larger than upside-down 9-inch glass pie plate. Fold pastry into fourths; place in pie plate. Unfold and ease into plate.

Spoon desired filling into pastry-lined pie plate. Unfold top pastry over filling; trim overhanging edge 1 inch from rim of plate. Fold and roll top edge under lower edge, pressing on rim to seal.

Tip: Roll dough in between two large pieces of plastic wrap to avoid sticking and to cause less mess.

FAMILY, FOOD AND THE FRIARS

APPLE PIE

Serves 6-8

2 pie crusts

1/3 cup sugar

1/4 cup flour

1/2 teaspoon nutmeg

1 teaspoon cinnamon

1/8 salt

8 cups peeled and sliced apples

1 teaspoon vanilla

2 tablespoons butter

Preheat oven to 425°F.

In a large bowl, mix sugar, flour, nutmeg, cinnamon and salt. Stir in apples and vanilla until apples are well coated. Line the bottom of a 9-inch pie pan with 1 pie crust. Pour in coated apples; dot the top of apples with 2 tablespoons butter. Line the top with second pie crust, pinch crust together at edges. Make 4 slices in the top of crust. Cover edge with 3-inch strip of foil to prevent excessive browning.

Bake 40 to 50 minutes or until crust is brown and juice begins to bubble through slits in crust, removing foil for last 15 minutes of baking. Serve warm if desired.

FRESH WHIPPED CREAM

Makes 3 cups

1 pint whipping cream

2 teaspoons honey (optional)

1 tablespoon vanilla extract

Beat in mixer on high or with whisk until desired thickness. Do not over beat. Top fresh whipped cream on coffee, hot chocolate, fruit or on any dessert.

PUMPKIN PIE

Pumpkin pie has always been synonymous with a Thanksgiving feast. My wife replaces milk in this recipe with heavy cream to add richness and flavor. Try it, and I think you will agree with her.

Serves 6-8

1 pie crust

1 cup sugar

1 teaspoon cinnamon

1/2 teaspoon cloves

1/2 teaspoon nutmeg

1/2 teaspoon ginger

1/2 teaspoon salt

3 eggs, well beaten

15-ounce can of pure pumpkin

1½ cups heavy cream

Preheat oven to 450°F.

Mix sugar, cinnamon, cloves, nutmeg, ginger and salt in a large bowl. Mix in beaten eggs. Stir in pumpkin. Gradually stir in cream.

Line a 9-inch pie pan with pie crust. Pour in filling. Place pie into oven and bake for 15 minutes. Reduce the oven temperature to 350°F, bake for 40-45 minutes or until middle of pie is set. Cool for 2 hours and serve or refrigerate, or just scoop it out hot like we do at home.

Top with fresh whipped cream before serving.

MOLTEN CHOCOLATE CAKE

Our restaurant has been preparing this recipe for years. It is especially satisfying with a scoop of vanilla ice cream. The secret to this recipe is not to overcook the cake so it will retain its gooey center.

Serves 6

5 ounces semisweet chocolate, chopped

5 ounces butter, unsalted

3 large eggs

3 egg yolks

1½ cup sugar

½ cup flour

Preheat oven to 350°F.

Butter six ramekins (¾-cup size) and set aside. In a double boiler, melt chocolate and butter; set aside to cool. Whisk together eggs and egg yolks. Whisk in sugar until mixed, add chocolate mixture and finally flour.

Evenly divide batter into ramekins. Bake until center of cakes are soft, about 11 minutes. Remove from oven and slightly cool. Run knife around edge and turn cake out onto dish. Serve warm with ice cream or fresh whipped cream.

Suggestions: If cakes are left over, refrigerate. When ready to eat, microwave for 45 seconds to soften the middle of the cake.

VANILLA ICE CREAM

Our family loves to make homemade ice cream, especially when we found out how simple it was to prepare. This recipe is a basic vanilla bean ice cream that can be tweaked; that is, you can add fruit, cocoa or any other flavorings. At our house we use honey instead of sugar.

I only have two requests when trying this recipe: make sure to use a fresh vanilla bean and use heavy cream instead of half and half or milk. You will be amazed at the richness and smoothness the cream adds to your ice cream.

Makes about 5 cups

   3 cups heavy cream

   1 vanilla bean

   6 egg yolks

   3/4 cup sugar (or substitute honey)

Heat cream in a saucepan. Cut the vanilla bean in half lengthwise and scrape out the seeds from the bean, adding them to the cream. Once the cream comes to a simmer, remove from heat, cover and let stand for about 30 minutes, allowing the vanilla to steep. Whisk the yolks and sugar together until well blended. Return the cream back to a simmer, take off heat and *slowly* add cream to egg mixture, whisking *constantly*. Return the mixture back to the saucepan and place over low heat. Cook slowly until custard thickens, about 5 minutes. Do not allow it to boil.

To test thickness: Dip spoon in custard and run your finger across spoon. If it leaves a path on the spoon, its ready.

Now it's time to crank up the ice cream machine. Pour the custard into the machine and follow the manufacturer's instructions.

Substitutions: Try adding coffee, cocoa or strawberries plus a few extra tablespoons of sugar.

STICKY DATE PUDDING CAKE WITH CARAMEL SAUCE

This recipe was borrowed from my mother-in-law (aka Grandma Mary), a wonderful cook and baker. This dessert appears to be unpretentious, but looks can be deceiving. It is love at first bite (don't forget the caramel sauce).

Serves 12

10 ounces pitted dates
1 cup water
1½ teaspoons of baking soda
3/4 cup of butter (1½ sticks)

1 cup of sugar
3 eggs
1 teaspoon vanilla
1/2 teaspoon salt
1½ teaspoons baking powder

½ teaspoon ginger
1¾ cups flour
Preheat oven to 350°F.

Simmer the dates and 1 cup water in large saucepan for 5 minutes; take off heat. Stir in baking soda and let cool for 20 minutes. Purée or mash the cooled dates in a food processor, blender or with a potato masher. Set aside.

In a mixer on high, mix together the butter and sugar until creamy. Beat in eggs one at a time; add vanilla. Beat until well mixed. In the butter mixture, alternate the dry ingredients, salt, baking powder, ginger and flour with the date mixture (start and end with dry). Beat until well incorporated.

Butter a 9 x 13 pan and place a sheet of wax paper or parchment on the bottom of pan buttering it also. Pour in mixture. If you want it very moist and sticky, place in a water bath (place pan with cake mix into a larger pan filled with halfway with very hot water) and bake. Bake for about 30 minutes. Do not over bake. Remove from oven, let cool. Cut into squares and serve with Caramel Sauce.

CARAMEL SAUCE

This makes a lot of sauce. You can easily cut the recipe down to half or a quarter.

Makes about 5 cups

1 pound of brown sugar (dark or light)

1 quart of heavy cream (organic seems to work best)
1/2 pound (2 sticks) of unsalted butter

Place all ingredients in a large, heavy-bottomed sauce pan (the mixture will boil up). Bring to a simmer, and cook for about 30 minutes or until desired thickness, stirring occasionally. Remove from heat, ready to serve *OR* stir occasionally, until mixture is totally cool. Place into jars. It will keep for a couple of months. Heat and serve as desired.

TIRAMISU

Tiramisu, which means 'pick me up,' is a classic Italian dessert. My mother has taken over the duties of preparing the tiramisu for the restaurant, and her first idea was to serve the dessert in a goblet, instead of preparing the dessert in its traditional cake form. It is much easier to serve and the presentation is outstanding. It took me a bit of coaxing to get the exact ingredients because Mom's recipe is as follows: a bit of sugar, some espresso, a few eggs, and don't forget the espresso.

You can't argue with success. Her tiramisu is delicious, and customers never tire of this classic dessert.

Serves 10-12

6 egg yolks

1 cup sugar

1 cup mascarpone cheese

2 tablespoons amaretto

2 cups heavy cream

22 ladyfingers cookies

1 cup espresso

Powdered cocoa for garnishing

In a large mixing bowl, beat egg yolks and sugar until thickened. Add mascarpone cheese and liquor and mix together. Set aside.

In another bowl, beat heavy cream until it forms a stiff peak. Gently fold whipped cream into egg yolk mixture. Spread thin layer of cream mixture on bottom of 2-quart serving dish or 10 goblets. Break ladyfingers in half, dip them into espresso and layer them on top of cream mixture. Repeat by adding another layer of cream and then adding another layer of espresso-dipped ladyfingers. To finish, garnish with powdered cocoa.

Refrigerate for about 4 hours before serving.

BISCOTTI

Biscotti are slices of cookies from a twice-baked cookie loaf. Italians love to dunk them in espresso, tea or even wine. These cookies can be made up to a month in advance and kept in a tightly sealed container.

Makes about 60 cookies

1 cup almonds

2¼ cups flour

1 teaspoon baking soda

Zest from 1 lemon

1 tablespoon anise seeds

1/2 teaspoon salt

3 large eggs

1 cup sugar

1 teaspoon vanilla extract

1 teaspoon almond extract

Preheat oven to 350°F.

Spread almonds in a small pan, and bake for 5-8 minutes until lightly toasted. Remove from oven and set aside.

In a large bowl combine flour, baking soda, lemon zest, anise seeds and salt. In a second bowl, beat eggs, sugar, almond extract, and vanilla with a mixer or whisk until thick, about 3 minutes. Mix in dry ingredients with egg mixture until well combined. The dough at this point will be soft. Flour your hands to keep the dough from sticking. Divide the dough into two equal pieces and carefully roll each piece into a log, about 2 inches wide and 12 inches long. Transfer each log onto a cookie sheet lined with parchment paper. Bake in oven for 30 minutes or until light brown.

Remove from oven and transfer the biscotti to a cooling rack for 10 minutes. Using a serrated knife, slice the log on a sharp diagonal (45 degrees) at ½-inch intervals. Stand the biscotti upright on the baking sheet, about 1/2 inch apart. Return baking sheet to oven and bake for 10-15 minutes or until crisp. Transfer biscotti to a wire rack to cool. Once cool, serve or store in an airtight container.

ACKNOWLEDGMENTS

I would like to thank my wife, Julia, for helping me accomplish this goal that I have had for years. Without her guidance, it would have never would have happened. I am fortunate to have met and married her; she continues to be my inspiration.

Thanks to my children, Gabby, Michael, Sofia, Veronica, Cecilia and Laura for being loving, caring, and obedient to their dad. They are my motivation and inspiration in life and bring such joy to everything we do together. My grumpiness was lifted and vanished once they became part of my life.

Thanks to my brother, Mark, for being a great business partner, and always being at my side through the tough times. Thanks, also, to my sister-in-law Kathleen, who gave the book a beautiful and stylish appearance with her pictures. I am forever grateful to Jim Reilly for coaching me in finishing this insurmountable goal. Thanks to Amy Kelley for editing the book and being a positive influence upon us. Thanks to Kristin Gawley for the time she spent on the beautiful cover.

I would also like to thank the customers at Gino's Trattoria, who push me every day to create fresh and delicious meals for their families.

None of this would be possible without my mom, Ivana, who brought me into this world and gave me the best childhood. She has been a true mentor and loving parent since the day of my birth. I love you, mom.

In memory of my dad, Vito, whose love and wisdom shaped me into the person I am today. Without his sacrifice and constant help, writing this book and accomplishing so many goals would not have been possible. My hope is that my children will look upon me as their role model as I once did towards him.

I would like to extend a huge thank you to my business partner/mentor, Adam Mitchell for expanding my mind and showing me the limitless possibility and also believing in my message and creating Gino's family . Thanks to Rob Kosberg for being part of Gino's Family and relaunching the book. Thanks to IPEC (Institute for Professional Excellence in Coaching) for the incredible 9 month journey to becoming a Certified Professional Coach. What an invaluable experience surrounded by positive, intelligent and caring people.

Thank you~

Julia & Gino

Gabriella, Michael, Sofia, Veronica, Cecilia, and Laura

41451404R00119

Made in the USA
Charleston, SC
28 April 2015